The Killer Instinct

It was April 24, 1973. The New York Rangers had just come out on the short end of a 4-1 score against the Black Hawks of Chicago. For the Rangers, that ended a season filled with disappointments, near-misses, might-have-beens—and more than their share of injuries.

But 1973 also saw the birth of a new breed of Rangers—tough, aggressive, hard-nosed. At no time was this more apparent than during the Boston play-off series. The Rangers body-checked, hip-checked, and gang-checked the Big Bad Bruins into an early vacation.

In 1974, the Rangers have the talent, the muscle—and the killer instinct—to bring the hockey gold back to New York. This is their story—past and present. And no one is better qualified to tell it than the Voice of the Rangers, Marv Albert.

Ranger Fever

MARV ALBERT
with
Stan Fischler

A Dell Book

DEDICATION

We authors, both of us, literally grew up in the "old" Madison Square Garden and would like to dedicate this book to the people who in our youth helped make us Ranger fans—the players, the broadcasters, and the press agents.

Since all of the names would be too numerous to mention we will list just a few who meant a little extra to us:

Don Raleigh, Buddy O'Connor, Chuck Rayner, Frank Boucher, Aldo Guidolin, Hy Buller, Wally Hergesheimer, Danny Lewicki, Andy Bathgate, Guy Gendron, Lou Fontinato, Dean Prentice, Gump Worsley, Andy Hebenton, Eddie Kullman, Max Bentley, Doug Bentley, Edgar Laprade, Stan Saplin, Herb Goren, Bert Lee, Ward Wilson, Marty Glickman, Pat Egan, Wally Stanowski, Pentti Lund, Ed Slowinski, Camille Henry, Bill Gadsby, Bill Ezinicki, Ivan Irwin, Jack Evans, Johnny Bower, Reg Sinclair, Tony Leswick, Grant Warwick, Jack Stoddard, Neil Colville, Frankie Eddolls, Jim Gordon, Win Eliot, and John Halligan.

MARV ALBERT
STAN FISCHLER

New York City
May 1973

CONTENTS

INTRODUCTION

by Bill Chadwick, member Hockey Hall of Fame

Years and years ago, before the center red line was introduced to pro hockey, there was a referee in the National Hockey League named Mickey Ion who was admired by all for his ability, courage and integrity. One night, prior to a game, Ion took one of his young protégés aside and gave him the reassurance that at one time or another every official needs.

"Look around you," Ion told the young referee. "There are fourteen thousand people in this building, but, once that puck is dropped, only one of them is sane—and that's the referee."

Having refereed sixteen years in the NHL and absorbed the slings and arrows of fans from Montreal to Chicago, I can assure you that there is more substance than saccharine in what Ion had to say. But I would like to add a small but significant amendment.

Nowadays at Madison Square Garden there is one other clear-minded, objective person in the building on hockey nights—and that man happens to be Marv Albert.

I thought I learned something about hockey during my long NHL association; something about officiat-

9

ing, playing, and coaching. But when I was named to the job of "color" man alongside Marv on the WNBC Radio play-by-play, I discovered that I was totally unaware of another dimension of the game.

A play-by-play broadcaster like Marv must be "in" the game for the entire sixty minutes of action. I learned by watching Marv that his job—done expertly as he does it—requires as much diligence, expertise, and concentration as any refereeing chore I've ever handled.

Which is why I owe a debt to this amazing young man. When I came along as his sidekick, I knew a heckuva lot about hockey but precious little about radio. That little round microphone in front of me was more intimidating than any of the five hundred players I had faced on the ice. I came into the radio business as raw as any rookie, and I might have flunked out at the end of my first season. But I had a terrific coach who had a lot of faith in me. He calmed me down, taught me what to look for, and when to talk about what I saw. In retrospect the thing I appreciated most about Marv in those early years was that he never told me what he wanted me to say. He gave me the nickname "The Big Whistle" and he had enough faith in my knowledge of hockey to let me take off verbally from there. Without Marv's encouragement I doubt that I would be where I am today.

Those were good years in the radio booth. We came along just about the time the Rangers began their climb to the upper regions of the NHL. We watched the "Gag Line" meld into one of the finest units in modern NHL history, and we shared the satisfaction of watching youngsters like Brad Park, Walt Tkaczuk, Steve Vickers, and Rod Seiling develop into first-rate competitors, all under the baton of manager–coach Emile Francis.

It has been a very gratifying experience—but not a completely satisfying one for me or for you Ranger fans. We are missing something, and that something, obviously, is the Stanley Cup. I thought we had it in 1972–73. But, as things turned out, our day did not come.

I have no doubt that it will come—and come a lot sooner than some of you think. In the meantime you can savor all the thrills and triumphs of past Ranger years in Marv Albert's book. He takes you back to the Roarin' Twenties—when big-league hockey all began in our town—and brings it all back: the Lester Patrick era, the first Cup win, the Cook brothers and Boucher, and on to the great prewar years of Watson, Hextall, Kerr, Shibicky, and the Colvilles, who won New York's last Stanley Cup in 1940. Then it's on to the difficult but exciting postwar era, right up to the arrival of Emile Francis and the achievement of new excellence for the Rangers.

There's never been a book like it, the complete Blueshirt chronicle. A book that has me and all hockey fans ravin' about the Rangers.

1. OUR DAY WILL COME

I was born and raised in Brooklyn and rooted for the Dodgers throughout my childhood. As much as anyone, I know the meaning of patience and fortitude, perseverance and grim determination. It took the Brooklyn Dodgers sixty-five years to win their first World Series. It has been thirty-four years since the Rangers last won the Stanley Cup. The Dodgers of the late forties and early fifties proved that, given time and quality, they would reward their rooters with a world championship. And so it will be with the Rangers.

There are those who, like old Brooklyn Dodgers fans, believe that it will be sixty-five years before the Rangers again drink champagne from the Stanley Cup.

I disagree.

Many of us believed that it would all happen during the 1972–73 season. The Rangers had a powerful team from goal to defense to the fourth forward line. But something was missing. That something, combined with a staggering and endless list of injuries, proved to be their downfall.

But it does not mean they will stay down, especially not in 1973–74; because too many good things happened last season to make a Rangers rooter anything but an optimist.

For one thing, Walter Tkaczuk developed from a relatively crude, uncertain center into one of the most poised, accomplished forwards in the National Hockey League. His left wing, Steve Vickers, broke a league scoring record within a month of turning regular. Despite a succession of injuries, Brad Park showed that he is still one–two with Bobby Orr as the best defenseman around. And, without question, Eddie Giacomin and Gilles Villemure remain unchallenged as the foremost goaltending combination since the Rangers owned Chuck Rayner and Jim Henry back in 1947–48.

More important, the Rangers got a monkey off their back. Up until April of 1973 the surest thing about an NHL season was that the New Yorkers' mortal enemies, the Boston Bruins, would bash them, bop them, and eventually beat them with goals, high sticks, spears, and other assorted weapons of destruction.

Even the Rangers themselves were fully aware of their nemesis. "I can't remember the last time we won a really big game against Boston," defenseman Park mentioned to me before the season began.

But 1972–73 was different. The Rangers opened with a decisive win over Boston at Madison Square Garden. They looked different and felt different. And as the season unfolded, the Bruins began to understand that these were no longer the light-armored

Rangers of old. I recall talking about the change.

"In important games against the Rangers," said hockey editor Mark Mulvoy of *Sports Illustrated,* "the Bruins always followed Battle Plan No. One. Intimidation they called it, and it worked something like this. In the first minutes of play the biggest, baddest Bruins charged, slashed, punched, tripped, battered, slammed, crashed, hooked, high-sticked or low-sticked the Rangers into the boards and onto the ice. Sometimes the Bruins even employed a combination of blows, like a high stick and a left to the jaw, to get their message across. After suffering these atrocities for about ten minutes the Rangers usually threw in the towel and adopted a pacifist posture as Bobby Orr led the Bruins to victory."

But by playoff time it was obvious the Rangers had started hitting back and that the Bruins had begun to move away. "You can only kick a guy so long," said Rangers forward Glen Sather. "After a while you've got to change your act." And so the Rangers, as one headline writer put it, were "97 POUND WEAKLINGS NO MORE!"

Precisely when the turnabout occurred is a matter of argument. Some observers say the change came at the start of the season. Others insist it was not apparent until the playoffs, and still others point to a game on the night of February 3, 1973, at Boston Garden as the decisive match.

At that time the Rangers had not won on Boston Garden ice, although they had been able to handle the Bruins in New York. More than that, it was a game right out of the big, bad Bruins mold. One report called it a "trench warfare game." Another called it a "mini-war."

Whatever the labels, Boston came out swinging, and just thirty-four seconds after the opening face-off, Bruins defenseman Don Awrey was penalized for board-checking Billy Fairbairn. With Bobby Orr leading the way, Boston successfully killed the penalty, and moments later Jim Neilson of the Rangers took two minutes for holding. Orr remained on the ice and launched the play that led to Ken Hodge's opening goal.

So far the script of previous Rangers–Bruins encounters was being followed to the letter. The game was hardly underway and already the Bruins had taken the lead. Now it was time for Act II, which is where the Bruins begin to pummel the Rangers into quiet submission. Act II began when Greg Sheppard of the Bruins squared off with Brad Park. Park hadn't even had a chance to get his gloves off when Terry O'Reilly came skating up from behind and rabbit-punched him to the ice. In the previous meetings between the teams, this was where the Rangers began to fold. But Brad Park was one of the new breed of Rangers.

"When O'Reilly crashed Park," said Mulvoy, "Park fought back. He didn't win the battle, but at least he retaliated."

And the Rangers kept retaliating—with fists and goals. When the final buzzer had sounded New York was on top, 7–3. The defeat must have meant something to the Bruins as well. Less than a week later coach Tom Johnson was replaced by Bep Guidolin.

Many of us thought that game would catapult the Rangers right into first place over Montreal and give the Blueshirts their first Prince of Wales Trophy (for finishing on top of the East Division) since 1942. They drew closer and closer to front-running Montreal until a Sunday afternoon in February when the Canadiens came to town.

This would be the first of a two-game, home-and-home series, the second game to be played at the Forum in Montreal. It was all Rangers right from the start. The seventeen and a half thousand spectators at the Garden reached a new high for decibel production as the New York defense actually prevented the high-scoring Canadiens from taking a shot-on-goal for the first 15:24 of the opening period.

Meanwhile the Rangers were breaching the Montreal defense time and again. Bruce MacGregor scored the game's first goal against rookie Michael Plasse, and Vic Hadfield's red light put New York two up as the teams skated out on the ice for the final twenty minutes of play. To every onlooker, the Flying Frenchmen appeared dead.

But the Canadiens are a proud team. They didn't quit, and soon Frank Mahovlich put Montreal on the scoresheet with a shot past Eddie Giacomin. Now it was 2–1, and the Canadiens pressed for the tie. Their exuberance was short-lived, as Claude Larose took a penalty for interfering with Rangers captain, Vic Hadfield. It looked great. The Rangers had their power play revved up and moved the puck into the Montreal zone.

The rubber went to Brad Park, one of hockey's

most expert point men. Normally he would have skimmed a pass across to his partner, Bobby Rousseau. But Rousseau had already darted toward the goal. Park was being pursued by defenseman Guy Lapointe of the Canadiens. Brad feinted with his head and shoulder and tried to send a pass to the goalmouth, but Lapointe stayed with him.

Lapointe's stick got in the way of the pass, deflecting the puck back in the direction of the Rangers' zone. Startled by the interception, Brad was unable to prevent the Montreal defenseman from outflanking him. Lapointe snared the loose puck and moved on a direct line for goalie Ed Giacomin.

As the menacing counterattack unfolded, I had wondered why Park tried such a dangerous maneuver in the first place. Later he told me his theory: "My plan was to get the pass to Rousseau, who was free near the Canadiens' goal. Even if the play failed, I figured I could get hold of anybody who had gotten away."

Brad managed to catch Lapointe and get a piece of the Montrealer, but a piece wasn't enough. Lapointe struggled free just as Giacomin moved from the cage to confront him.

"The second Lapointe got away from me," said Park, "I saw Eddie get ready for him. Maybe I could have fouled him or pulled him down (and get a penalty shot called against the Rangers), but I felt it would be better for Eddie to handle him."

In situations like this the goalie has two options: he can remain within his goal area and play the shooter in traditional fashion or he can gamble and skate all the way to the blue line hoping to beat the shooter to the puck. Giacomin, who likes to gamble, charged toward the loose puck. As it turned out, this was the most unfortunate play of the regular season for the Rangers.

Seeing Giacomin and realizing that he was off-balance and unable to make a normal play, Lapointe desperately speared the puck, pushing it goalward.

Giacomin's stick blunted the shot, sending it back to Lapointe. It hit the Canadien's shinpad and rebounded past the helpless Rangers goalie. Even then the situation could have been saved if one of Giacomin's teammates had been able to get to the puck in time.

But Park was the only Blueshirt available and he was hopelessly horizontal. The nearest skater was Chuck Lefley, the Montreal rookie, who had trailed the play on the right wing. In a second Lefley leaped at the puck and shoved it into the vacated net.

The score was tied, 2–2, and remained that way until the final buzzer. Montreal had retained its four-point lead over New York, leaving the Rangers' dressing room looking like a morgue. By the time I arrived after the broadcast, the dressing room was half empty and so quiet you could hear a puck drop.

"Sure it was a tie," Park conceded, "but to us it was as bad as a defeat. Everybody feels down because we had been working so hard for the win."

Like Park, I felt bad for Giacomin. He had gambled and lost. Should he be faulted on the play? I wondered about that and finally decided to put the question to Montreal's All-Star goalie Ken Dryden, who had been injured and had watched the game from the press box.

"Giacomin didn't make a mistake," said Dryden. "He did the right thing under the circumstances. What turned it around was Lapointe's incredible play."

Then I asked Montreal's coach Scotty Bowman. He left no doubt about the matter. There were no goats, only a hero—Lapointe. "First he blocked Park's pass," said Bowman, "then he had to wrestle Park for the puck going down the ice. A lot of guys would have stopped and done something else with the puck. After all, Park does happen to be one of the best defensemen in the league.

"As they raced down the ice, I was hoping they would both fall down in a heap and Lefley would be able to pick up the loose puck. But Giacomin came out of the net. I wouldn't say he made a mistake, because how many times do you figure to get to the puck first and have it bounce off one player right to another? This time it did, and we got an easy goal."

It left the Rangers four points out of first with another game against Montreal, this time at the Forum. New York was in trouble. Captain Vic Hadfield had broken his thumb against the Canadiens and right wing Bruce MacGregor suffered a fractured ankle. Ranger fans began thinking the club was skating under a black cloud, but general manager-coach Emile Francis refused to get depressed.

"I don't think we're jinxed," Francis told me. "I don't believe in stuff like that. We're in a rough game where you have to expect injuries. It just seems that we get more than our share. As for the upcoming game with the Canadiens, it's important, but I don't think it will decide first place."

This time Francis was wrong. The Canadiens dominated the Rangers, built up a 5–0 lead, and coasted to a 6–3 victory. From that point on Montreal pulled further away from the pursuing Rangers and Bruins in the standings.

The Rangers finished third, behind Montreal and Boston. Judging from critical reports throughout the league, New York might just as well have forfeited their opening-round Stanley Cup test against the big, bad Bruins. It was not that the press was anti-New York, but rather that they remembered May 1972, when the Bruins whipped the Rangers in six.

According to Frank Orr of *The Toronto Star* it would be just as dismal for the Rangers in 1973. "Once again," said Orr, "Boston holds all the advantages—extra home game, psychological edge, no injuries, momentum, Phil Esposito—and Bobby Orr."

I couldn't argue with him. The Bruins had roared past the Rangers in the homestretch to capture second place. Esposito was hot and Orr was hotter. What's more, the Bruins had added goalie Jacques Plante to their lineup, giving them two experienced goaltenders for the playoffs, Plante and Ed Johnston.

At forty-four, Plante was participating in his sixteenth NHL playoff. Bruins coach, Bep Guidolin, decided to start Plante in the opening game at Boston Garden. Francis gave Giacomin the Rangers' assignment. Unlike the critics, Francis betrayed no pessimism about the outcome of the series. I met with him before the start of the first game and he explained why he believed his club could upset Boston.

"We can play the Bruins any way they want to play," said Francis, "slick or tough. Steve Vickers has shown that we can fight with the best of them."

And so he had. In addition to his unanimous decision over Don Marcotte on February 3, Vickers staged a toe-to-toe draw with Ken Hodge in March which was just as decisive. "The Bruins had an aggression advantage," said Orr, "but they cooled it after Vickers stood his ground."

The Rangers realized they had to penetrate ancient Jacques Plante as early as possible. Plante was a money goalie and a smart goalie, but he was also old and possibly nervous. I got that impression from talking with him before the series began.

"Sure I'll be nervous," Jacques told me. "I was nervous in my first playoff game, and that was twenty years ago. Do you remember that?"

I recalled that the Canadiens had played the Black Hawks. It was April 1953 and Chicago had a three-games-to-two lead in the Stanley Cup semifinals. Gerry McNeil was the regular goalie, but he had played so poorly that coach Dick Irvin decided to try the rookie Plante.

"That night," Jacques told me, "I was so nervous I couldn't even tie my skates. But Rocket Richard calmed me down. He walked over to me in the dressing room and held out his hands. They were shaking like two leaves. He said, 'Jacques, don't be embarrassed, everybody gets the jitters in the playoffs.'"

Plante won that game, and Montreal went on to beat Chicago in the 1953 series. But a lot had changed in the twenty years since then. Jacques had played for the Rangers and then Toronto before moving to Boston. With the Maple Leafs he was just an average goalie. After coming to the Bruins he was sensational again.

"It's a lot different with a team like Boston in front of you," Plante explained. "When I was with Toronto I could count on maybe two or three goals from the offense. The Bruins can explode. So I know if I make a mistake or give up a goal, maybe it won't be critical."

Plante had just written a book about goaltending. He was extra-analytical. I wondered how he felt about the Rangers. "New York," he said, "has balance and experience. The team had to make adjustments because of Hadfield's and Rod Seiling's injuries. But Hadfield will be back and they'll have settled lines to throw at us. And don't forget that Ron Harris has improved his defense while filling in for Seiling."

At the time I virtually ignored his remark about Harris. He had come to New York from Atlanta in the deal for Curt Bennett and was regarded as a fifth defenseman who could never be expected to star against Boston. Yet Plante saw fit to mention Harris.

Two games later I knew the reason why. Ron had demolished Bruins left and right as the Rangers upset Boston, 6–2 and 4–2, on Boston Garden ice. In the second game Harris had collaborated with Vickers to sandwich Phil Esposito with a crunching bodycheck that tore the knee ligaments of the NHL's leading

23

scorer. Esposito was finished for the playoffs, and so, it appeared, were the Bruins.

"The coffin," said coach Guidolin, "is still open, but they're getting the hammer and nails ready."

It remained open after the third game, which Boston won at Madison Square Garden. Ed Johnston had replaced the shaky Plante in the net and rookie Greg Sheppard starred up front. Guidolin decided to use Johnston again in the fourth game, but this time the Rangers beat him and went back to Beantown hoping to wrap up the series on enemy ice.

To a Ranger fan, defeating the Bruins is a joyful enough prospect. But the thought of knocking the Boston sextet out of the playoffs in Boston Garden was heady stuff. After all, the Rangers had not beaten the Bruins in Cup play since 1940.

"I think we can do it," said rookie Steve Vickers. "I got that feeling after we beat them in Boston on their own ice in the first game."

The Bruins started thirty-five-year-old rookie goalie Ross Brooks. Within thirty-eight seconds of the opening face-off Vickers had beaten him. Boston came back and scored twice, but Vickers got his second goal before the first period had ended, and then Bruce MacGregor had put New York in the lead once more.

"I knew we had them," said Vickers, "because we were outskating them, outchecking them, outhitting them, and outsmarting them. I was surprised that we could do it so easily."

Brooks was yanked after the first period and replaced by Johnston. The Rangers couldn't have cared less. Walt Tkaczuk captured a loose puck with sixty-one seconds left in the second period and beat Johnston. That made it 4–2 New York. From there it was the Rangers in a walk. They scored two more goals in the third period, while the Bruins got one, and danced off the ice with a 6–3 victory. They had defeated the defending world champions in such convincing style that the Bruins could only stare in disbelief when I visited their dressing room moments after the final siren.

"I never thought they'd beat us," said goalie Johnston. "After we passed them in the regular season I thought they had had it. But I guess that had inspired them more than anything. They wanted to prove they could come back and beat us."

As you might have guessed, the Rangers dressing room was bedlam. Eddie Giacomin seemed to be shouting the loudest and rookie Vickers appeared to be taking the win with the most cool.

"It was very satisfying to beat them," said Vickers, who had scored a three-goal hat trick in the fifth game. That was enough for him, but not enough for his teammates. They seemed to generate more and more enthusiasm as they left the dressing room and headed for the airport and their triumphant return to New York. Even I hadn't bargained for what was to follow, although I played a significant part in making it happen.

As the fifth game drew to a close and it had become apparent that the Rangers would win, I mentioned on the air several times that the Blueshirts would be flying back home immediately after the game. It would be a heartwarming gesture, I suggested, if Ranger rooters came out to LaGuardia Airport to welcome them. Sal Marchiano and Bill Chadwick reinforced this thought on TV.

When I made the announcements I expected a handful of fans would make their way to the airport. After all, it would be after midnight, it would be difficult to get to the airport, and it was a dreary night—not the kind of conditions that normally drew the average spectator out of his house. But, I discovered, Ranger fans are not average spectators. They are superfans.

As our plane touched down, the players were singing their last chorus of "Good-bye, Bruins, Good-bye Bruins, we hate to see you go." The doors of the jet opened and we poured out to a sea of faces that I would estimate exceeded five thousand. Extra police and airport security personnel tried to contain them as we deplaned, but the crowd wanted a piece of their heroes. Soon it appeared that the throng would get out of hand.

We all managed to get off the field, but the trouble started when the players tried to get to their taxis and automobiles. For a few seconds I was worried the police might lose control of the crowd. But this mini-riot was limited to enthusiastic shoving and pushing, punctuated by cheers of "ED-DIE, ED-DIE" for goalie Ed Giacomin.

All of the players finally made it safely to their cars and cabs and disappeared into the night as Emile Francis shook his head in disbelief. "It just shows," said the boss of the Blueshirts, "there are a lot of people behind us."

These people hoped and prayed that the Rangers would march all the way to the Stanley Cup. The Chicago Black Hawks figured to be an easy mark. A year earlier, with Bobby Hull in the lineup, the Hawks went down to defeat in four straight games. Why should it be different this year?

Only rookie Steve Vickers seemed to sense trouble ahead. "We lose the psychological advantage," Steve told me. "Since we knocked off Boston, we'll be favored to beat Chicago."

New York was favored, and *looked* the part as the Black Hawks were routed in the opening game at Chicago Stadium. When coach Billy Reay's team rebounded for a win in the second game, the Rangers weren't all that concerned. And neither was I. After all, the game *was* in Chicago and the Rangers *did* overcome a three-goal deficit before losing. "They'll be thinking about the way we came from behind," said captain Vic Hadfield.

Vic was wrong. Chicago didn't think about anything but winning, and that first loss was the beginning of the end. Chicago skated on to Madison Square Garden ice and beat New York in the third and fourth games.

All of a sudden the Rangers were playing against the Black Hawks the way the Bruins had played against the Rangers in the opening round of the playoffs. Chicago wiped the Blueshirts out of the Cup competition in the fifth game. Once again the Rangers were pulled up just short of the end of the rainbow. The 1972-73 season ended with a whimper instead of a bang. The year that was supposed to be wasn't, and for several weeks thereafter the Rangers wondered just what had gone wrong.

But all that is past. A new season is upon us, and once again hope springs that the Stanley Cup will soon proudly reside at Madison Square Garden.

2. BIRTH OF THE BLUESHIRTS

The birth of the Blueshirts, alias the New York Rangers, was a sheer accident. No more, no less. When professional sports went big-time at the conclusion of World War I, hockey was not on the list. To the average New Yorker, ice hockey was a game reserved for Canadians and for the upper-class collegians who played at the cramped St. Nicholas Rink in mid-Manhattan about a mile and a half north of the present Madison Square Garden.

Organizing a big-league hockey team must have been the last thing on the mind of George Lewis, "Tex," Rickard, a Texas-reared promoter who had come East in search of athletic gold. For one thing, Rickard knew nothing about hockey, and for another his world revolved around boxing. Yet that very same Tex Rickard would father the New York Rangers.

It happened because of a newspaperman and a bootlegger, of all people. And it happened in spite of Tex Rickard.

Shortly after moving from Texas to New York, Rickard and a group called the "Six Hundred Millionaires" joined forces to build a new sports palace on

Eighth Avenue and 50th Street in Manhattan to replace the old Madison Square Garden.

Rickard's idea was to feature boxing at the "new"
Garden and fill it at other times with such diverse
events as the circus, track meets, and six-day bicycle
races. Hockey was not even considered, and the proof
of that was in the blueprints, which called for an over-
hanging side balcony that eventually was to obstruct
one-quarter of the hockey rink from the fans' view.

Neither Rickard nor his millionaires had bargained
for the intrusion of Bill McBeth, a New York newspaperman whose roots were in his native Canada, where
hockey was king. When McBeth learned about the
proposed "new" Garden on Eighth Avenue, he immediately realized that it would be a natural place to
stage hockey games.

"Bill had often said that if he had the money he
would back a team of his own," said the late Frank
Graham, a pal of McBeth's and himself an acclaimed
columnist. "But only a few people paid any attention
to him."

Undaunted, McBeth went looking for angels. The
year was 1925 and money was easy to come by; particularly if you knew William, "Big Bill," Dwyer, a
native New Yorker who was making a bundle as a
bootlegger. Fortunately for the future of hockey in
Manhattan, McBeth and Dwyer were friends, very
good friends.

"Why don't you buy yourself a hockey team?" Mc-
Beth suggested. And before Dwyer could ask his pal,
"What's a hockey team?" McBeth explained that (a)
he could obtain a major league club for almost a song,

(b) it would enhance Dwyer's reputation as a sportsman, which wouldn't hurt his bootlegging, and (c) hockey was played on ice by six men on each side and it was the fastest game on earth.

"Okay," said Dwyer, "but where do I find one?"

McBeth had done his homework. He knew the National Hockey League was on the lookout for more American franchises. Boston's Bruins had become the first American club in the league, and now the NHL was trying to peddle the Hamilton (Ontario) Tigers to the highest bidder.

"The club you want," said McBeth, "is in Hamilton, Canada. You can buy it for about seventy-five grand."

Using a chap named Tom Duggan as intermediary, Dwyer bought the Hamilton franchise in time to operate it in New York during the 1925–26 season. By any standard Dwyer—and McBeth and Duggan—had made a brilliant move, for theirs was not a patchwork expansion team but an accomplished club with stars and savvy from top to bottom. A colorful, redheaded Irishman named Tommy Patrick Gorman was chosen to manage the Tigers, who were renamed the "Americans."

Tex Rickard, who still didn't know a hockey puck from a bowling ball, was pleased anyway to have a full-time client at his new Garden. "Rickard," said Frank Graham, "didn't know anything about bigleague hockey until opening night. But it wasn't Bill McBeth's fault."

Opening night for big-league professional hockey in New York took place amid much fuss and fanfare on

December 15, 1925. The revered Montreal Canadiens provided the opposition, and the affair was treated with all the pomp and circumstance that New Yorkers could produce in the Roarin' Twenties.

Frank Graham, who attended the opener, remembered it vividly: "It was a great show. The West Point band was there and so were the Canadian Governor-General's Foot Guard band, Mayor John F. Hylan, and seventeen thousand other people, including society dolls in mink coats. Rickard was amazed!"

The Americans lost the game, 3–1, but the spectators didn't seem to mind. They filed out of the spanking new arena oozing with excitement over this speedy Canadian sport and the colorful players on both teams. In one night hockey had made it in the Big Apple.

McBeth helped his cause by taking a job as press agent for the Americans. With unconfined enthusiasm he touted the virtues of these virile Canadians. Billy Burch was labeled the "Babe Ruth of Hockey," and Joe Simpson became the "Blue Streak from Saskatoon."

Rickard, the promoter who at first had treated the idea of major-league hockey with benign neglect, suddenly became infatuated with his exciting new tenants, especially after they played to several capacity houses. Under the terms of the Americans' contract with the Garden, the team would pay the Garden more money as the crowds grew bigger and bigger. On certain sellout nights the Garden made more money than the Americans.

Dwyer couldn't have cared less. He didn't even

mind the Americans' fifth-place finish, which deposited them out of the playoffs, nor did he care that expenses for the team were high. After all, Big Bill's bootlegging business was booming, and his hockey team helped make him respectable in New York society.

But Dwyer did care about one thing, and he cared a lot. Following the end of the 1925–26 season he heard rumors that the Garden was so impressed with ice hockey's drawing potential that the arena corporation was on the lookout for a hockey team of its own which would compete directly with the Americans. Dwyer was furious because he didn't care for competition and, more important, he believed the Garden was trying to pull a fast one.

"Bringing in a new team," said Graham, "was in violation of a promise to Dwyer that the Garden would not bring in a second hockey team. But his protest was in vain since he had nothing in writing to prove it."

Meanwhile Rickard's forces moved speedily ahead with their plans for a new team, to be called the New York Rangers. They hired a young Torontonian named Conn Smythe to organize the team. Volatile and foreign to compromise, Smythe quarreled frequently with the Garden brass. After only one month on the job he was replaced by Lester Patrick, a regal-looking athlete who had been a splendid defenseman and later became the architect—with his brother, Frank—of the Pacific Coast Hockey League.

The loss of Smythe could have been a tragedy for the Rangers, because he was and would continue to prove himself a hockey genius. But the arrival of Patrick was a bit of uncanny luck since Lester, too, had one of those rare hockey brains, and proved it as soon as the 1926–27 season got underway. By the halfway point in the campaign the Rangers were on top of the five-team American Section of the NHL with a 12–7–3 record, while the Americans held third place in the Canadian Section with an 11–12–0 mark.

Much of Patrick's success could be credited to Smythe, who had assembled most of the Rangers before he left the Garden. The first line, featuring stylish Frank Boucher at center between the Cook brothers, Bill and Bun, took the league by storm, with Bill eventually emerging as the league's leading scorer in that rookie year for the Rangers. Hal Winkler and Lorne Chabot split the goaltending for New York. Ching Johnson and Taffy Abel were the rocks on defense.

There were many scintillating skaters on that first Ranger team, but none captured the imagination of the Garden crowd like the brothers Cook and Frank Boucher. They moved across the rink with the grace of figure skaters and passed the puck with radar-like accuracy. It was difficult to choose among them. Bill was the crackerjack shot, Bun had the brawn, and Boucher all the class in the world.

"Boucher became a center such as the league seldom has known," wrote Dink Carroll of the *Montreal Gazette,* "and a darling of the gallery gods and of the rich folk in the promenade seats as well. He would take the puck away from the enemy with the guile and smoothness of a cannon picking the pockets of yokels at a country fair, then whisking it past the enemy goaltender or slipping it to Bill or Bun."

Without question Boucher was the cleanest player ever to lace on a pair of skates in the NHL. He won the Lady Byng Trophy so many times—seven in eight seasons—the league finally *gave* it to him.

Oddly enough the one fight Boucher had in his entire NHL career took place in the Rangers' very first game on Madison Square Garden ice, November 16, 1926, against the Montreal Maroons, the Stanley Cup champions. "They were big," wrote *New York Times* columnist Arthur Daley, "and they were rough. Every Maroon carried a chip on his shoulder."

The chips became heavier when Bill Cook took a pass from brother Bun and scored what proved to be the only goal of the night. Fortified with a one-goal lead, the Rangers began counterattacking with their bodies and fists. Balding Ching Johnson would drop a Maroon to the ice and then grin his very special trademark smile that delighted the Garden crowd. Huge Taffy Abel hit every Montreal skater in sight, and soon the rink was on the verge of a riot.

Up until then the gentlemanly Boucher, who had once been a member of the Royal Canadian Mounted Police, had minded his business and stayed out of trouble. But "Bad" Bill Phillips, one of the most boisterous of the visitors, belabored Boucher with his elbows, knees, and stick at every opportunity. "The patient Boucher," wrote Daley, "endured the outrages until a free-for-all broke out."

At that point Boucher very discreetly dropped his

stick, peeled off his gloves, and caved in Phillips' face with a right jab. The Maroon badman slumped to the ice, whereupon Boucher politely lifted him to his feet and belted him again. When Boucher lifted Phillips for the second time, the Montrealer grabbed his stick and bounced it off Boucher's head, thus ending the fight.

To some fans that opening-game brawl was mere small potatoes compared with the clashes that were to come whenever the Rangers and their bitter rivals, the Americans, met. Nobody ever captured the "feel" of the excitement better than Frank Graham:

"To one who was a part of it," wrote Graham, "mind pictures of it linger. Sound pictures, with over-tones of music . . . of laughter . . . of angry bellows . . . of snarls and curses . . . of flashing skates and rushing feet and whacking sticks . . . of dark accusations by rival coaches that referees and goaltenders and goal judges were intimidated by gangsters who had bet on the Americans and wished to insure their bets.

"The entrance of the Rangers into New York had created a rivalry equaled only by that between the Giants and Dodgers in baseball. The nights these teams played at the Garden were gay nights . . . mad nights . . . and riotous nights.

"The opposing players, warming up, skating back and forth, the crowd humming, the players uncon-sciously falling into the rhythm of the music . . . and then the game. The star-spangled Americans, the blue-shirted Rangers hitting head-on. Skating . . . driving . . . hooking . . . slashing . . . checking . . . checking into the boards. The shrill blasts of the refer-ees' whistles . . . The roars and hoots and moans of the crowd . . . The fist fights in the galleries . . . The night that the Americans having lost a close game, some of their adherents chased one of the referees down Fifti-eth Street, calling him a thief and threatening to kill him if they caught him. Which, fortunately, they didn't."

It was a meaningful year for the Rangers in many ways, but most important they finished first in the American Division, while the Americans were fourth in the Canadian Division. After only one season the Rangers were established as the class team of New York, while the Americans were regarded as a colorful collection of skaters who would excite you and irritate you and make you love them, but would never win a championship. After only one season behind the bench Newsy Lalonde quit as coach of the Americans, while Lester Patrick was riding high as the leader of the Rangers. For Tex Rickard—the Rangers were named after Tex's Rangers—it was a marvelous season.

Amazingly the Rangers finished their first season eleven points ahead of second-place Boston. But in the last regular season game, on March 26, 1927, at Madison Square Garden, the Bruins surprised the Rangers with a 4–3 win, a victory that would have significance in the Stanley Cup playoffs to come. After defeating Chicago in the opening round, the Bruins came head-to-head with the Rangers, who had drawn a bye in the first round. In those days the teams played a two-game, total-goals series in the early Cup rounds, which is the way it was then for the Rangers and Bruins.

The series opened on April 2, 1927, on Boston Gar-

den ice, and what followed was a defensive classic—
the brand of tight play that would be known as "kitty-
bar-the-door" or typical playoff hockey. Neither team
would give an inch from the forwards to the defense
to Lorne Chabot and Hal Winkler in the goals.

"Shore [Eddie] and Hitchman [Lionel] were im-
pregnable on defense for Boston," wrote Charles L.
Coleman in *The Trail of the Stanley Cup*, "while
Abel and Johnson were equally as good for the
Rangers." The score reflected the action. Neither
team managed a goal and the teams entrained for
New York tied in the total goal series, 0–0.

In the first playoff game ever staged at Madison
Square Garden the Rangers were a disappointment,
although Bill Cook opened the scoring in the first
period. But the Bruins rebounded in the second period
when Jimmy Herberts tied the count, and Hitchman
and Harry Oliver beat Chabot to give Boston a 3–1
victory and the series.

It was a dismal ending to what had been a glorious
first year for the Rangers. Despite it Lester Patrick
was secure in the knowledge that he had a superb
team and Tex Rickard was confident that owning the
Rangers was virtually a license to print money. They
both were right and the following season proved their
points.

3. LESTER PATRICK AND THE GOLDEN AGE

Any team that could finish in first place after only one season of operation had to be awfully good or awfully lucky. The Rangers had both factors going for them. They were good because Conn Smythe had done the vital spadework unearthing first-rate players for the Blueshirts. And they were lucky to have signed Lester Patrick when Smythe walked out on them.

Like Smythe, Patrick was a truly fabulous character. Born in Drummondville, Quebec, Lester and his brother, Frank, learned their hockey in Montreal, where the Patrick family moved when Lester was ten years old.

Both were natural athletes who won headlines playing hockey for McGill University in Montreal. As pros they skated for such bygone teams as Westmount, Montreal, and Brandon before accepting an offer of $3,000 apiece from millionaire Martin J. O'Brien to play twelve games for the Renfrew (Ontario) Millionaires, then the newest entry in the National Hockey Association.

Renfrew was a boom town, suddenly made rich by mining interests. O'Brien had plenty of money and signed such aces as Newsy Lalonde and Cyclone Taylor to skate side by side with the Patricks. Those were fun times in pro hockey, but the Patricks were visionaries as well as players. They realized that hockey was the coming sport in North America.

In 1911, when their father, Joseph Patrick, a millionaire lumberman, retired, Lester and Frank decided the time had come to make their dream of a Pacific Coast Hockey League come true. With their father's financial support, Lester and Frank organized the new league and built Canada's first artificial ice rink in Victoria, British Columbia.

They soon built another rink in Vancouver and put franchises in Seattle, Spokane, Portland, Victoria, and Vancouver. By 1914 an East–West playoff for the Stanley Cup had begun, and the Patricks had reached the pinnacle in big-league hockey.

Among his other accomplishments, Lester became president of the Pacific Coast League and learned the administrative ropes the hard way. Lester liked to recall the problems he suffered with referee Mickey Ion, who later became one of the NHL's foremost officials. One night when Ion was refereeing a game in Seattle, he took exception to a front-row fan armed with a large megaphone. Whenever Ion skated by, the fan would assail his ears with an assortment of curses. "Ion finally stopped the game," Lester recalled, "and demanded that the megaphone or the fan be removed. Ion won the battle this time, but the next time he appeared in Seattle the fans really gave it to him. There were six thousand fans at the game and it seemed that all six thousand of them had brought megaphones."

The moment the megaphones blared, Patrick noticed that Ion had stopped play. He wanted all the megaphones confiscated and removed from the stands. Lester walked down to rink-side and beckoned the referee to the boards.

"For Heaven's sake, Mickey," said Patrick, "you can't get all six thousand megaphones."

"If I don't get the megaphones," said Ion, "the game will end here and now!"

Patrick had no choice but to back his referee, whose decision was made known to the crowd. They were compelled to give up their megaphones. As Lester fondly recalled, the crowd *did* give Ion the megaphones, although obviously not the way he wanted them. "They threw them at him," said Patrick. "When all the noise had ended, Mickey was standing at center ice, knee-deep in megaphones."

Patrick and Ion usually saw eye to eye. Once, when Lester's Victoria Cougars were playing Saskatoon, Ion's decision against Saskatoon enraged Newsy Lalonde, who was managing the Saskatoon club. Lalonde berated Ion at every opportunity, apparently failing to realize the referee was carrying a rather large bell in his hand instead of the traditional whistle. Patrick noticed the bell and asked his captain, Clem Loughlin, to find out why the referee was using a big bell instead of a whistle. Ion looked toward Lalonde and told Loughlin, "Hell! You can't wallop anybody with a little whistle."

In 1924, at the age of forty-two, Lester coached and managed the Victoria Cougars to a Stanley Cup triumph over the Montreal Canadiens, three games to one. In that same year NHL franchises were awarded to the Montreal Maroons and the Boston Bruins, and a year later to the Pittsburgh Pirates and New York Americans. Patrick realized he couldn't match the salaries the big-time Eastern moguls were offering players. He knew that the time of the Pacific Coast League had ended, so he sold his entire roster to the new owners in the East and planned to move to California and retirement.

After nineteen consecutive years managing and playing hockey, Lester Patrick was ready to take a vacation. Then Conn Smythe walked out on the Rangers and Lester was called. He took the first available train East, and the new era in hockey for New York City had begun.

If Patrick's first year with the Rangers was remarkable, what could he possibly do for an encore? The 1927-28 season would hold the answer.

Having finished first, Patrick believed he had a winning combination. Lorne Chabot remained in goal with Ching Johnson and Taffy Abel manning the defense. The Cook brothers and Frank Boucher were designated the first line, while Lester selected a second line of Murray Murdoch, Paul Thompson, and a newcomer, Alex Gray. The relief defensemen were Leo Bourgeault and Pat Callighen.

The Rangers opened the season on November 15, 1927, at Toronto with a 4–2 victory. Smiling Ching Johnson scored two goals and his grin was wider than ever.

It was clear that Lester had another powerhouse. But so did his rival in Boston, Art Ross. The Bruins didn't open as well—they played to a 1-1 tie with Chicago—but they closed with a flourish, beating the Rangers out of first place by four points.

In the playoffs Patrick's skaters went up against Pittsburgh in a two-game, total-goals series. The first match was at Madison Square Garden, and the Rangers took it in a walk. Boucher, Johnson, Bun Cook, and Alex Gray were the goalscorers in a 4-0 triumph.

The teams changed roles in the second match. This time Pittsburgh carried the play and won the game, 4-2, but New York captured the series, six goals to four. The Rangers now advanced to the semifinals against the Boston Bruins, again a two-game, total-goals series. The first game, on March 31, 1928, would be the final contest of the season on Garden ice no matter how the Rangers fared. In those days the Ringling Brothers, Barnum & Bailey Circus had precedence over the hockey team, and the circus was about to move into the Garden.

Both teams played outstanding hockey in the opener, which ended in a 1-1 tie. Frank Frederickson scored for the Bruins, Boucher for the Rangers. The series moved to Boston for the final contest, and this time there was no stopping the Patrickmen. They swarmed over the Bruins defense, scoring four times to Boston's one, and took the series five goals to two. New York had reached the Stanley Cup finals in its second season and now faced the awesome Montreal Maroons on April 5, 1928, at the Forum.

Deprived of their home ice, the Rangers considered offers to play their "home" games in either Boston or

Detroit, but the offers were refused. Every game would be played on the unfriendly ice of Montreal's Forum.

The Maroons, bulging with such stars as Nels Stewart, Babe Siebert, and Hooley Smith, blanked the Rangers, 2–0, in the opening game. Hockey is rough today, but in the Roarin' Twenties it was even rougher. Players hated each other, coaches hated each other, and owners hated each other. The hatred manifested itself in the second game when Ranger goalie Lorne Chabot was wounded by a shot that smashed into his head above the left eye. Chabot was through, but the Maroons insisted that he finish the game. If not Chabot, then another Ranger. Montreal refused to loan New York a goaltender.

It was then that forty-five-year-old Ranger manager Lester Patrick staged one of the most startling scenes in hockey history. Patrick laced on the pads midway in the game and held Montreal to a 1–1 tie through the seven-minute mark of sudden-death overtime. It was then that Boucher captured the puck, weaved through the Maroon defense, and scored the winner at 7:05 of the sudden death. Now it was 1–1 in the best-of-five series.

But the Maroons were hardly dead. They shutout the Rangers, 2–0, in the third game. All the Montrealers needed was another win for the Cup. With the partisan Forum fans roaring behind them this seemed like a simple enough task—if some way could be found of disposing of Boucher. But the Maroons had not yet discovered a suitable method. Boucher scored the one and only goal of the fourth game for New York, and the series was tied at two apiece.

The Maroons had won the Cup two seasons earlier, and an early goal in the fifth and final game indicated they would soon own another, especially when the Rangers were penalized early in the match. By this time Lester Patrick had replaced the injured Lorne Chabot with a goalie named Joe Miller. The mere mention of the name "Joe Miller" brought smiles to the faces of all concerned, especially the opposition.

"He'd been named 'Red Light Miller,'" Boucher explained, "because he had played for the New York Americans. They had a losing team in those days, so naturally Joe was a losing goalkeeper. Frankly, I never thought he was that bad and, as things turned out, he was just magnificent in the last game."

Down a man, the Rangers had Boucher at center, hoping he could stickhandle long enough to permit his teammate to return. The Maroons had moved into the Ranger zone. The puck began to skip from man to man as if it were being conducted by an invisible string. Suddenly the string was broken. Boucher had the puck. He moved over the center circle and down the back of Montreal defenseman Mervyn, "Red," Dutton, who later became National Hockey League president, and still later one of Canada's foremost millionaires.

"I knew his weakness," Boucher remembered. "If you pushed the puck through his legs, instead of watching you he'd look down at the puck. I tried the puck and, sure enough, he looked down. By the time

45

he looked up again, I was around him. I picked up the puck, skated in on Clint Benedict, and flipped it into the right-hand corner."

The Rangers' troubles were far from over. Again they were penalized and again Boucher was dispatched to the front. This time Boucher controlled the puck at center ice. "I played it off the boards," he said, "hoping to pick up my own rebound and keep it in our possession."

But he shot it too far ahead; so far, in fact, that it tantalized Maroon defenseman Dunc Munro. The Montreal player raced for the rubber, which was sitting almost midway between the two opponents. "I was watching him," Boucher added. "He came out seriously for about fifty feet. Then I could almost hear him thinking, 'By God, I can't get there in time.' He seemed to stop in one motion, and then he changed his mind and went for the puck. By this time I was there. I just swooped over to one side, let him go by, and then I had the whole ice to myself."

Maroon goalie Benedict had as much chance as a chipmunk against a panther in an enclosed cage. Boucher roared in and put the puck in exactly the same place he had earlier in the game. The Rangers were ahead, 2–1. They had visions of the Stanley Cup.

Enraged at themselves, the Maroons counterattacked with fury. In one assault Russell Oatman took a pass from Bill Phillips and beat goalie Miller to seemingly tie the score. But referee Mike Rodden, in a courageous move, waved his hands, signifying "no goal." The referee claimed that Phillips was offside on the play.

At this point the Montreal fans unwittingly helped the Rangers. They showered the ice with missiles, protesting Rodden's decision. "This proved to be a relief for the hard-pressed Rangers," wrote Charles Coleman in *The Trail of the Stanley Cup*. "They secured a welcome breather while the deluge of rubbers, bottles, hats, scarves, and paper was being removed."

The respite was just the tonic the Rangers needed. Once the ice was finally cleared they blunted the Maroons with ease and protected their slim lead until the bell sounded to end the game. The Rangers had won their first Stanley Cup!

Patrick had assembled the nucleus of a juggernaut that would last for many years, although its Cup-winning potential was not fully realized again until April 1933. The Rangers finished second in the American Division during the 1928-29 season and faced their hated Garden rivals, the Americans, in a two-game, total-goals opening round.

As Rangers–Americans battles went, this was a classic; a 0–0 tie highlighted by superb goaltending from John Ross Roach for the Rangers and Roy, "Shrimp," Worters for the Americans. Unbelievably the second game also ended in a 0–0 draw, necessitating a sudden-death overtime. Just ten seconds from the thirty-minute mark Butch Keeling of the Rangers took a pass from Paul Thompson and flicked the puck past Worters for the victory.

The Rangers went all the way to the finals before succumbing to the Bruins, two games to none. It was a disappointing ending for Patrick and it hinted at more troubles to come the following season, when the Blueshirts dropped to third place and were eliminated from the Cup semifinals in two straight games by the Montreal Canadiens.

Not until the 1931–32 season did the Rangers really regain their early superiority, finishing first in the American Division, seven points ahead of runner-up Chicago. But the Cup eluded them once more when the Toronto Maple Leafs knocked them out of the finals in three straight games.

At the start of the 1932–33 season Patrick still had his team built around the Cook brothers and Boucher. Ching Johnson shared the defense with Earl Siebert, but the goaltending underwent a switch with Andy Aitkenhead replacing John Ross Roach.

The Depression was at its low ebb and attendance throughout the NHL suffered. The Rangers cut ticket prices by one-third: the best seats in the house were reduced to two dollars while the cheapest went for forty cents. On December 22, 1932, Col. John Hammond, the man who hired Lester Patrick, resigned as Rangers president and was replaced by none other than Lester himself.

Although the Rangers finished third in the American Division, their record of twenty-three wins, seventeen losses, and eight ties, for fifty-four points, equaled that of first place Toronto in the Canadian Division. This time the Rangers could not be stopped. They whipped the Canadiens eight goals to five in a two-game, total-goals quarterfinal series and then knocked off the Detroit Red Wings in a similar series, six goals to three. That pitted them against the Maple Leafs in a best-of-five final.

Paced by the Boucher line, New York lost only one game—the third, 3–2—enroute to their second Stanley Cup championship. The victory was sealed by Bill Cook's sudden-death overtime score in the fourth game. That was the last Cup celebration for the Blueshirts for several years, but it didn't end the Rangers' winning ways. They played capable hockey, although they lacked the little extra zip to go the route. On top of that the stars—the Cooks, Boucher, and Johnson—were getting old.

Patrick realized that changes had to be made. He was one of the first to develop a farm system, and by the mid-thirties fresh, new talent like goalie Davie Kerr; defensemen Ott Heller, Art Coulter, and Babe Pratt; and forwards Neil and Mac Colville—a latter-day replacement for the Cooks—Alex Shibicky, and Phil Watson had replaced the old guard.

Although he knew that he would be ridiculed for the move, Patrick also signed his son, Lynn, an outstanding left wing, to the team after much soul-searching. Lester feared that he would be charged with nepotism, but Lynn stopped the critics by simply playing outstanding hockey.

The young Rangers began coming into their own in the 1937–38 season, when they finished second to Boston in the American Division with twenty-seven wins, fifteen losses, and six ties, for sixty points, which was more than the fifty-seven points amassed by Toronto, leaders of the Canadian Division.

The Rangers didn't win the Cup that year but they were participants in what was one of the most exciting hockey games ever played in New York. The date was

March 28, 1938. Once again it was New York vs. New York—the Rangers vs. the Americans at Madison Square Garden. It was the deciding game of the first-round Stanley Cup series and New York City was in an uproar over the rivalry. Unlike the Rangers, their Garden rivals had never won the Stanley Cup and had become sentimental favorites among a large portion of the city's sporting crowd—many of whom were in line at dawn that day to obtain the precious tickets for the dramatic match.

The Garden bulged to overflowing when the rival goalies, little Davey Kerr for the Rangers and huge Earl Robertson of the Americans, skated out onto the ice. It was 8:30 p.m.—and nobody in the building would have dreamed at the time that the teams would still be skating against each other long after midnight!

Neither team scored in the first period. The Rangers took command in the second as Alex Shibicky and then Bryan Hextall whipped the puck past Robertson. Many in the crowd of 16,340 believed the Americans were dead. One of their fans picked up his coat, walked out of the arena and across 49th Street, where he sat down to a drink at the bar.

An hour and three drinks later he turned to the bartender and inquired about the final score. "Final score?" snapped the bartender. "Why that game is still on!" At which point the fan grabbed his ticket stub and dashed back to his seat in the Garden.

Sure enough the Americans had tied the game on goals by Lorne Carr and Nels Stewart. It was 2–2 at the end of regulation time, and now sudden death was upon them. Neither team scored in the pulsating first overtime period, although it was clear that offense was emphasized. Surely the game would be settled before the second sudden death had ended.

"To the grandstanders it was almost unbelievable," according to one report, "but neither team could mount a successful scoring drive in the second over-time session either. Surprisingly, few people departed by midnight even though it appeared that the game might go on indefinitely. Here and there spectators rushed out to the lobby refreshment stands—which finally ran out of food—but most of the huge crowd was on hand when the end came."

Limp from excitement, the fans thought the result had been sealed in the third overtime when Americans defenseman Joe Jerwa beat Rangers goalie Kerr—only to see his shot clank off the goal post and bounce to the front of the goal crease, where it was smothered by defenseman Ott Heller.

Following that play Cecil Dillon of the Blueshirts zigzagged his way through the Americans' defense and tested Robertson with a sizzling drive. But the big guy stopped it with his pads. Once again the momentum shifted to the Americans. Sweeney Schriner burst into the clear after taking a perfect pass from Art Chapman. Goalie Kerr steadied for the shot, but Carr lifted it high over the net and into the crowd—and another overtime period had ended.

Many in the crowd had begun to wish that an earlier incident had not been "corrected" by the officials. The star of the incident was a female Rangers fan who had rushed down to the goal judge's area following a scramble in front of the Americans' net and pushed the red light buzzer signaling a goal.

"The goal judge, Charles Porteous of Montreal, nearly swooned," wrote an observer. "Players wrangled and referees Bert McCaffrey and Ag Smith had a merry time restoring order."

When the fourth overtime started, most of the spectators anticipated a close-checking style of kitty-bar-the-door hockey. The clubs charged at each other with renewed vigor. Less than half a minute had elapsed when the Americans took control of the puck. It was Jerwa to Chapman, who had set up Schriner so perfectly before. This time the puck went to Lorne Carr, and he made no mistake. The shot beat Kerr and the Americans had won the longest hockey game ever played on Garden ice.

Time of the game: one hundred twenty minutes and forty seconds! The Amerks went on to blow the best-of-three semifinal round to Chicago, dropping the second and third games after winning the opener, 3–1.

Patrick's building program continued apace. He added his younger son, Murray, to the defense, and like his older brother, Murray—known affectionately as "Muzz"—proved himself a capable big-leaguer. In the 1938–39 campaign the Rangers finished second to Boston, losing to the Bruins in a stirring best-of-seven opening playoff round, four games to three.

Lester Patrick was getting on in years and realized that he couldn't coach the team forever. To those closest to the Rangers the choice of a successor seemed obvious. Frank Boucher had been a Ranger since the opening season and played center until the end of the 1937–38 campaign. He had won the Lady Byng Trophy seven times and led the team in scoring five times. If Lester Patrick was Mister Hockey in New York in the front office, Frank Boucher was Mister Hockey on the ice. He was everybody's favorite—the fans, the newspapermen, and the players.

By the 1939–40 season it was official. Boucher had become coach of the Rangers. His team was big, tough, fast, and inventive. "I'd encourage suggestions," he said. "The boys would come up with them and then we'd practice the new ideas."

One was the box defense, whereby the four players killing a penalty arranged themselves in a "box" formation in front of the goaltender. A more "sensational" one, as Boucher put it, was an offensive penalty-killing combination. Instead of playing a tight defensive game, the Rangers would try to turn a disadvantage into an advantage. It was the beginning of modern forechecking. "When we were a man short," Boucher recalls, "we'd send out three forwards and one defenseman and we'd forecheck in their own end. This worked so well, we scored more goals over the season than were scored against us during the penalty-killing."

On November 23, 1939, the Rangers played a 1–1 tie with the Canadiens. From that point on they won fourteen games and tied five for a nineteen-game unbeaten streak, a club record. Boucher believes it could easily have been extended to twenty-five; but these Rangers were too smart for their own good.

"We were playing Chicago in the twentieth game of the streak," says Boucher, "and playing rings around them. It was the kind of game we should have won hands down, but for some strange reason we couldn't score a goal and were down, 1–0, going into the third period."

During the intermission Boucher came up with another revolutionary idea. If the Rangers hadn't tied the score—they were convinced Chicago wouldn't score another goal—by the final minutes, New York would pull goalkeeper Davey Kerr, but not in the usual way. In most cases a team waits for a whistle and a face-off before replacing the goaltender with a sixth skater. This, of course, enables the opposition to prepare for the extra man. "We decided," says Boucher, "that it would be better to put in the goalie without making it obvious—to do it on the fly."

Chances are it would have worked, but Boucher neglected to inform Lester Patrick of the plan. Normally this wouldn't have mattered, since Lester didn't occupy the bench. But this night in Chicago he was at rink-side with the players. Lester was mistrustful of the Chicago timekeeper. When the clock turned to within minutes of the end he got off the bench and sat down next to the timekeeper, who was located between the Black Hawk and Ranger benches.

"By this time," said Boucher, "we had the puck in their end. The signal was given for Kerr to come off the ice and the extra forward to go on. And that's exactly what happened. Nobody in the rink realized what happened but my players—and then Lester, except he didn't know that Kerr was removed."

Believing that Boucher had made the mistake of allowing too many men on the ice, the frantic Lester beseeched Boucher to remove the sixth skater before the referee saw him.

"Paul Thompson, the Black Hawk coach, heard him," Boucher recalls, "and when he saw six men in his zone he started screaming. We were about to put the puck in the net when the referee blew his whistle to give us a penalty. Then he turned around and saw Kerr was out and there shouldn't be a penalty at all. But it was too late. The attack was stopped and we lost the game, 1–0."

Boucher's mighty Rangers won their next five in a row for an overall record of twenty-four victories or ties in twenty-five games. They defeated Boston, four games to two, in the Stanley Cup semifinal round and faced Toronto in the finals.

Three of the games—including the final two—went into sudden-death overtime, and in each of the contests the Rangers scored the winner. With the series tied 2–2, the last three games were scheduled for Toronto ice because Madison Square Garden was unavailable. The Rangers won the fifth game, 2–1, at 11:43 of the first overtime, the sixth at 2:07 of the first overtime—and the Stanley Cup.

4. GREAT MOMENTS FROM THE NON-CUP YEARS

The Rangers' last Stanley Cup came on April 13, 1940. That year was the high-water mark of hockey interest in New York City as the storm clouds of World War II began gathering across the world. Already many NHL stars had enlisted in the Canadian Armed Forces, and a steady stream would continue to join the Army and Air Corps as the war continued.

On the home front the war between the Rangers and the Americans was, unfortunately, winding down. Once the only big-league hockey team in town, the Amerks had hit dark days. With the end of Prohibition Big Bill Dwyer lost his fortune—and his hockey team. By 1935 Red Dutton, a marvelous hockey player and the son of a rich Canadian, took over the team and maintained a degree of class.

"Red," said Frank Graham, "was one of the greatest players of any sport and, happily, he remained one of the greatest guys ever connected with any sport. . . . Unfortunately he caught up with the Americans too late to do much good. Although he was still one of the best defensemen in the league, he was like the hounds in a road show of *Uncle Tom's Cabin* of whom a critic said, 'The hounds were excellent but they lacked support.'"

The year the Rangers won their last Cup, the Americans finished in sixth place. In the 1940–41 season they were dead last with an awful record of only eight wins, twenty-nine losses, and eleven ties. When the 1941–42 season began the Amerks were on the ropes. Out of desperation their name was changed from New York Americans to Brooklyn Americans, although they still played on Garden ice. It was, as one observer put it, a dodge that fooled nobody.

At season's end the Rangers were on top of the league and the "Brooklyn" Americans were on the bottom. Surprisingly their record was much improved —16–29–3—over the previous season. They had developed a remarkable young goalie, Charlie Rayner, and two promising forwards, Ken Mosdell and Harry Watson.

But the war was reaching its height by now and the nucleus of the Americans' roster had joined the armed forces before the 1942–43 season began. On September 28, 1942, the Americans' franchise was officially pronounced dead by the NHL governors at their meeting in Toronto. In a stirring obituary for his favorite team, journalist Graham concluded, "The Americans are dead and gone and so are Bill McBeth, who dreamed them up, and Big Bill Dwyer, who made McBeth's dream come true."

Instead of capitalizing on the Amerks' demise, the Rangers seemed to be incorporating the worst traits of their deceased neighbors, namely, losing. Of course the Blueshirts had an excellent excuse; the cream of

Lester Patrick's crop had left for the war, led by Muzz Patrick, one of the first hockey players to enlist.

In one season the Rangers plummeted from first to last. By the 1943–44 season the Rangers had lost so many bodies to the war effort that Frank Boucher himself, who had not played since the 1937–38 season, felt obliged to put on the Rangers uniform again.

Naturally Boucher tried to reactivate his glorious number seven jersey. But center Phil Watson had the number and defied the boss. "If I gave you back number seven," Watson reasoned, "it would jinx me. I've got me a good number. You look around and you can probably find one too."

After a brief search Boucher came up with number fourteen. He played in fifteen of the fifty games and, remarkably, averaged almost a point a game. He scored four goals and ten assists before calling it a career. Boucher went behind the bench, and what he saw there should have been enough to convince him it was better for the nerves to be back on the ice. Quite simply, the Rangers were a dreadful team, particularly on defense and in goal.

Their goaltender, Ken, "Tubby," McAuley, finished the season with a goals-against average of 6.20. On January 2, 1944, he was bombed, 13–3, by the Bruins at Madison Square Garden and on January 23, he lost 15–0—a league record never equaled—to the Red Wings at Olympia Stadium in Detroit. To some spectators the Rangers looked infinitely worse than the Americans at their worst!

And no relief was in sight, at least not until the war's end, when the stars of the last championship team would return to gain still greater glory. Or so everyone hoped.

By the 1945–46 season the war veterans drifted back to the NHL, Alfie Pike, Alex Shibicky, Neil and Mac Colville, and Ott Heller were among the returnees, along with the first Ranger to go, Muzz Patrick. But instead of a glorious return the Ranger fans were treated to an almost pathetic sight. The heroes of prewar days had aged and their skills had been dulled by the long absence from the ice. When the 1945–46 season ended they were still buried in last place, a full ten points out of fifth.

If there was one consolation it was in the play of Chuck Rayner, the former Americans goaltender obtained by the Rangers. His spectacular spreadeagle saves and boundless courage were an inspiration to the Blueshirts and their loyal fans, who had packed the Garden throughout the dismal war years.

It was clear to Frank Boucher, who had taken over the helm of the Rangers, that new blood was needed to replace the prewar heroes, who had lost their spark and their style. One of the first of the "finds" was provided by Al Ritchie, who scouted western Canada for the Blueshirts. He recommended a small, bulldog type forward named Tony Leswick to the Rangers, and within two years "Tough Tony," as he was known on Broadway, had become the team's leading scorer.

The turnabout from chronic loser to consistent winner didn't happen overnight, but Leswick went a long way to pump fighting blood into the postwar Rangers. He not only led the team in scoring during the 1946–47 campaign but was just as useful as the supreme needler of the opposition and "shadow" of its leading scorers.

"Leswick gets under your arms and between your legs," said Toronto Maple Leafs defenseman Garth Boesch. "He annoys the life out of you!"

More than anyone, the fabulous Maurice, "Rocket," Richard of the Montreal Canadiens had the life annoyed out of him by Leswick. Once, at the Montreal Forum, Leswick needled the Rocket, and Richard swung his stick at Leswick. The referee sent Richard to the penalty box with a two-minute minor. Leswick didn't stop there and pestered the Rocket throughout the match. With just a minute remaining, Richard blew up again, and again the referee sent him to the penalty box.

"The second time around," said Leswick, "he kicked me. I shouted back at him, 'You ever do that again and I'll put the lumber to your head.' "

At game's end, Richard bolted from the penalty box and charged Leswick, whereupon the two of them brawled for several minutes while teammates and officials attempted to separate the pair.

The Richard–Leswick feud continued for several years. "Mostly," said Leswick, "I'd call him a homer. Sometimes I'd get a little tougher than that."

One day a reporter asked Richard what he thought of the hard, little Ranger. "I have nothing good to say about Tony Leswick," the Rocket shot back. "He is not a hockey player. What does he do out there? He talks and talks. He is a talker, not a hockey player. He talks to you. Half the time he thinks I am mad. I am not mad. I am laughing at him because he thinks he has made me mad."

Of course Richard wasn't Leswick's only target. Once, in a playoff game against the Detroit Red Wings, he was given a two-minute penalty, followed closely by a two-minute penalty to teammate Nick Mickoski. The timekeeper, whose duty it was to wave inmates back onto the ice when their penalty time had expired, became Leswick's target.

"Tony chattered and argued about the time he was to return to the ice," said Rangers publicist Stan Saplin, "and so confused the timekeeper that he was allowed back in the game long before his penalty time was up."

Leswick wasn't Boucher's only postwar find. His scouts had unearthed a trio of sparkling players in western Canada and placed them with the Rangers' farm team in the Eastern Hockey League, the New York Rovers, who played their home games on Sunday afternoons at the Garden. The Rovers were immensely popular, particularly with young fans. But they were never more popular than in the years immediately after World War II, the years of their "Atomic Line."

Centering the unit was Calvin, "Ginger," Gardner, a long, lanky skater who was as tough as he was smart. Gardner was flanked by industrious René Trudel and Church Russell. As a trio they were as flashy in their own way as the old Boucher Line was in theirs. After giving them a brief fling in the 1945–46 season, Boucher elevated the entire line for the 1946–

47 campaign as the Rangers' secret weapon.

Unfortunately nobody told them what the secret was to making it in the big time. With the exception of Gardner, who became a solid center, the Atomic Line, secret weapon that it was, failed to lift the Rangers into a playoff berth in the 1946–47 campaign. On the bright side, though, they did come close —close enough to frighten the Montreal Canadiens and close enough to precipitate the biggest brawl ever on Garden ice, if not in the entire league.

It happened on the night of March 16, 1947. After battling gallantly for a playoff spot, the Rangers were about to be eliminated by the Canadiens in the second of a brutal two-game series. It was late in the game when rambunctious Kenny Reardon, a Montreal defenseman, skated toward the Ranger goal, only to be felled by a high stick.

Reardon twitched in pain as he was led to the first-aid room. But in order to get there he first had to pass the Rangers bench and three rows of angry fans who were delighted to see him bleed. As Reardon made his way past the Rangers, one of them shouted an obscenity at him, while a fan threatened to punch the Montrealer.

Suddenly the Rangers bench rose as one to see what was happening. Watching the action from across the rink, the Canadiens players thought the whole Ranger team was about to pounce on the injured Reardon. Taking a cue from coach Dick Irvin, the Canadiens raced across the rink to engage the Rangers.

Within seconds the players from both teams spilled out onto the ice, swinging their sticks like machetes.

Even the most temperate and innocent skaters found themselves engulfed in the madness. One of them was Herbert, "Buddy," O'Connor of the Canadiens, who had spent only twenty-four minutes in the penalty box in his entire six years in the NHL. O'Connor decided to stay out of the fight, but he was right next to a teammate who whacked Rangers defenseman Bill Juzda over the head with his stick.

The enraged and dazed Juzda whirled around and swung wildly, his club cracking across O'Connor's face. The blow broke Buddy's jaw. Up in the radio booth Bert Lee, the voice of the Rangers at that time screamed, "It's a riot! IT'S A RIOT!!" Which is precisely what it was. The fight went on into the night until a squad of New York City policemen finally calmed the exhausted skaters.

Ironically, the most damaged player on the ice, O'Connor, was traded to the Rangers the following season and was to become one of the outstanding forwards in Ranger history. It also was one of the steals of the century, since the Rangers obtained the slick-passing center for only $6,500. "I'll do the best I can for you," O'Connor told Boucher, and his best turned out to be sensational.

In the opening game of the 1947–48 season the Rangers met the Canadiens at the Forum, and O'Connor was hailed as a Ranger as much as he ever had been as a Canadien. "When Buddy was traded," said one writer, "the citizens of Montreal reacted as though chunks had been chipped from the Forum ice and dropped down their backs."

O'Connor showed them why. His sparkling plays

made the difference as the Rangers upset the Canadiens, 2–1. When Buddy scored his first goal for the Rangers against Montreal, the rabid French-Canadian fans set up a din that usually was reserved for the great Maurice Richard. "They don't know what they're yellin' for," said O'Connor's teammate Phil Watson.

But they knew all right. And with each game it became more evident that Buddy O'Connor would not only be a Rangers star, but would lead them back to the playoff grail for the first time since 1942, six long years ago. He played in every game of the sixty-game schedule and scored in forty-three of the sixty games. From December 17, 1947, to January 28, 1948, he scored in sixteen out of seventeen games! His record for the year was twenty-four goals and thirty-six assists, and he led the league in scoring until the final day of play when Elmer Lach, his former teammate on the Canadiens, beat him out by one point.

A few weeks after the season was over the sportswriters voted O'Connor the Hart Trophy as "the player adjudged to be the most valuable to his team" and the Lady Byng Trophy as "the player who exhibits the best type of sportsmanship and gentlemanly conduct combined with a high standard of playing ability during the season."

Most satisfying of all was the fact that O'Connor meant the playoffs to the Rangers. The proof was in the standings. Buddy's former club, the Canadiens, finished out of the playoffs in fifth place, four points behind New York. Buddy, along with the other Rangers, performed valiantly in the semifinal Cup round against the Red Wings. They lost the first two games on Detroit ice, returned to the Garden and won the next two, but lost game five in Detroit and the sixth and last match back at the Garden.

The Rangers were on the threshold of what *New York Times* writer Joseph C. Nichols described as potentially the "Golden Age of the Garden ice crew."

The ingredients were there, to be sure. In addition to Chuck Rayner in goal, Boucher boasted another first-stringer, Jim Henry—who just happened to be Rayner's closest friend—giving the Rangers a head-start for what later was to become the two-goalie system.

After many years of coaxing, Boucher had persuaded Edgar Laprade, a lithe and intelligent center, to turn pro, and Laprade had come into his own as a first-rate star. The defense, anchored by Bill Moe, one of the best of the submarine-checkers, Frankie Eddolls, Neil Colville, and Bill Juzda, was solid if not sensational. Up front the Atomic Line still had hopes of achieving stardom, while forwards such as Eddie Kullman and Ronnie Rowe fortified the playoff chances for 1948–49.

Then it happened.

The jinx that was to cast a black cloud over the Rangers' fortunes so often in years to come struck the Blueshirts and struck hard. In the midst of an excellent training camp, the Rangers were enroute to an exhibition game from their base at Lake Placid, New York. They traveled in private automobiles in those days and one of them was involved in a terrible accident. Laprade, O'Connor, Eddolls, and Moe were seriously injured and taken to a hospital. "New York's pennant hopes," wrote Barney Kremenko of the *New York Journal-American,* "were smashed."

Boucher did everything possible to patch up his line, and before the year was finished forwards Jackie Gordon and Buck Trainor were elevated from the minors and defenseman Allan Stanley was purchased from Providence for the astounding figure of $80,000. By the final weeks of the season the Rangers had eight rookies on their roster, a record for the NHL.

The auto accident had taken its toll. O'Connor missed the first fourteen games of the season and never recaptured the scoring style he had displayed the previous season. Eddolls remained inactive until December thirty-first and didn't regain his old-time form until the final weeks of the season.

The 1948–49 Rangers finished last again, but the rebuilding program showed promise, and a season later the flowers of the Blueshirt farm system finally blossomed in all their splendor.

Paced by Leswick and Laprade, the club climbed to fourth and engaged second-place Montreal in the first playoff round. The Canadiens were heavy favorites to win the series, but Boucher's boys were hitting their peak. Young Pentti Lund completely overshadowed Rocket Richard and led the Blueshirts to a startling four-games-to-one triumph over Montreal.

The unexpected victory catapulted the Rangers into the Stanley Cup finals for the first time in ten years. Their opponents were the vaunted Detroit Red Wings, one of the strongest teams in NHL history. If that wasn't problem enough, the Rangers also had to contend with the fact that *none* of their home games could be played at Madison Square Garden because the circus was back in town. Maple Leaf Gardens in Toronto was designated the Rangers "home" rink.

The series opened at Olympia Stadium in Detroit and, judging from the events that night, could have closed then and there. The Red Wings were positively awesome as they routed New York, 4–1. Patrick was so furious with his club's play he ordered goalie Emile Francis up from his New Haven farm club to join the team for the second game in Toronto.

Precisely what changed the texture of the Rangers' attack overnight cannot be determined for sure, but the New Yorkers were a new team. They clearly defeated Detroit, 3–1, before a very friendly Maple Leaf Gardens crowd that had adopted the Blueshirts as their very own.

Unfortunately the Rangers couldn't sustain their momentum. They lost the third game of the series, 4–0, and fell behind, two games to one, as the series switched back to Olympia. Ominous suggestions that the Rangers would fold and leave for an early vacation were immediately dashed in the fourth game. Fighting from behind, the Rangers overcame 0–2 and 2–3 deficits to tie the score at 16:26 of the third period and force a sudden-death overtime.

It had been a particularly grueling series for center Don Raleigh. Nicknamed "Bones" by his teammates for his conspicuous lack of flesh, Raleigh was "mod" twenty years before his time. He lived alone on Staten

Island; wrote poetry; grew a mustache; and always gave the impression that one more turn on the ice would be his last.

But Raleigh was on the ice as the clock passed the eight-minute mark of the first sudden death. He took a pass from bulky linemate Ed Slowinski and, as he was falling, swiped the puck past a beaten goalie Harry Lumley. The Rangers had tied the series at two apiece.

Now the Red Wings were reeling. They fell behind, 1–0, in the fifth game and appeared to be doomed to a Chuck Rayner shutout when Ted Lindsay tied the score with less than two minutes remaining in the third period. Once again it was time for sudden death —and Bones Raleigh.

An unlikely hero if ever there was one, Raleigh wasted little time in his second dramatic sudden-death effort. Only a minute and a half had elapsed when he took a pass from teammate Eddie Slowinski and beat Lumley with a ten-foot drive. The amazing Rangers had taken a three-games-to-two lead in the series. One more win and they owned the Stanley Cup!

In the sixth, and what appeared to be the final game of the series, the Rangers led by two goals after the first period. But Detroit came battling back, and when the final siren shook the stadium, the Rangers found themselves on the short end of a 5–4 score.

The seventh and final game played at Olympia on April 23, 1950, has gone down in history as a classic. On the one hand there were the underdog Rangers, gamely trying to pull off a rare ice wonder, and on the other there were the proud Red Wings, determined to capture the Cup before the roaring Detroit fans.

Yet those who jammed the venerable Motor City ice palace couldn't help but admire the Rangers, who had become affectionately known as the "Hitless Wonders," because of their low goal average. "But," said Stan Saplin, then Rangers publicist, "at that point in the series they looked and acted the part of champ."

All the hockey world—except for those fans in the Detroit-Windsor area—had taken the Rangers to their hearts. They had suffered more than sixty injuries during the year and had lost the valuable services of defenseman Wally Stanowski, and still they carried the battle.

"For a period of fifty-two minutes and thirty-four seconds on that night of April 23," said Saplin, "all they had to do was score one goal and they would have been champions of the world."

Just as in game six, the Rangers grabbed a 2–0 lead, but couldn't hold it. Detroit tied the score, 2–2, then Buddy O'Connor, looking like the Buddy O'Connor of old, scored to give New York a 3–2 lead. The time was 11:42 of the second period. More than half of regulation time had expired. If only Rayner could hold on . . .

But the Red Wings muscled their way into the Rangers' zone, and before the Blueshirts had a chance to exult over their lead, Jimmy McFadden had beaten Rayner and the score was tied at 3–3.

The score remained deadlocked throughout the third period. A goal in sudden death would decide the game. "Even Detroit's most loyal adherents," said Saplin, "admitted the Red Wings overcame the Rangers on sheer power."

Yet they couldn't beat Rayner. An entire twenty-minute sudden-death period had elapsed and the Rangers were still alive and kicking. Once they had actually beaten Lumley; only a half-inch separated them from the Cup, but the shot hit the goal post and bounced harmlessly to the side.

In the second sudden-death period the Red Wings revved up their attack. But eight minutes passed without a goal. Rayner had been at his punting, sprawling, spreadeagled best. Then, at last, the end came—in its way surprisingly peaceful.

The face-off was deep in Ranger territory. Facing up ice was Buddy O'Connor, taking the draw for New York. Opposite him was George Gee, a tall, strong Detroiter who whispered some advice to teammate Pete Babando seconds before the puck was dropped for the critical face-off. Babando nodded and moved slightly to the right, just as Gee had suggested. It was the turning point in the series.

Gee beat O'Connor to the puck and skimmed a pass to Babando. The move was right out of the textbook, just as the two had planned. As soon as the puck reached Babando he cracked his wrist and the black rubber soared goalward. A phalanx of multicolored bodies separated an anxious, crouching Rayner from the puck.

"Bonnie Prince Charlie," as they called Rayner, couldn't see it coming. He had to anticipate where it might surface, and he anticipated wrong. It beat him to the right corner of the net, snuffing out the last flicker of Cup hopes, which Bones Raleigh, Ed Slo-winski, and all the Rangers had helped keep alive for so long.

And so the twenty-fourth season in the Rangers' history went into the books. It was a glorious season, to be sure, but missing one big, fat item—the Stanley Cup.

Nevertheless, the Rangers emerged from the 1949–50 season the real heroes of pro hockey. "The fact that a member of the Red Wings scored that goal," said one observer, "in the final overtime game and not a man in a Blue Shirt did not lessen the grand attainments of the gang of skaters who weren't supposed to have it—but did!"

5. ON THE REBOUND

The 1950–51 season was the Rangers' Silver Anniversary, their twenty-fifth year in the NHL. Hopefully it would be a winning year, culminating with a Stanley Cup triumph. But it wasn't to be.

The first blow was struck by Lynn Patrick, who had so ably coached the club to the 1950 Cup finals in Detroit. Criticizing New York City living, Patrick gave up the Ranger coaching job and, after saying he was moving to the West Coast, turned up in Boston, where he signed with the Bruins as their bench leader. His replacement, ex-Ranger Neil Colville, couldn't find Patrick's winning formula.

After seventeen games of the Silver Anniversary season the Rangers had won but a single game. The situation became so critical that manager Boucher even took a gamble and invited a psychiatrist, Dr. David F. Tracy, to hypnotize the Blueshirts into thinking they were winners. The doctor failed by one goal.

With each defeat, more and more pressure surrounded Boucher. Early in December 1951 he declared that he would resign his position if the Blueshirts failed to make the playoffs. When Boucher made the announcement the Rangers were in last place, eight points out of a playoff spot. To a man his players rallied around their beloved—I'm not being corny, Boucher truly was beloved—manager.

In the space of a month they won seven games, lost two, and tied three. All of a sudden they found themselves in third place. How they did it was debatable. Certainly Boucher's bold message motivated them. But there were other factors. That was the season when restaurateur Gene Leone produced his "magic" elixir in the famed black bottle.

The Rangers were once again the most exciting athletes in the NHL, and the playoffs seemed imminent. But history repeated itself and again disaster struck. With half a season to go, crack center Edgar Laprade was sidelined with a fracture of the left ankle. Goalie Chuck Rayner was afflicted with just about every imaginable injury, and the team's leading goal-getter, Nick Mickoski, suffered a shoulder dislocation.

Yet they held on right down to the homestretch and appeared to have the playoff berth clinched if they could beat the Canadiens at the Garden. Emile Francis had replaced the injured Rayner in the nets that night and had a comfortable lead as the third period wore on. But the Canadiens suddenly got hot when a rookie named Claude Robert scored a freak goal—the only goal of his entire NHL career—and the Montrealers stormed the New York net. With a minute to go Montreal had pulled to within a goal of tying the game—and a tie would virtually squelch the Rangers' playoff hopes.

The face-off was to the right of Francis. Montreal

won the draw and the puck skimmed to the blue line, where ancient defenseman Butch Bouchard heisted a long shot that seemed easy enough for Francis to handle. But the little goalie seemed to misjudge the drive. It hit him in the shoulder and bounced into the net. The game ended in a tie, and a few days later the Rangers were eliminated from playoff contention.

Boucher, as promised, handed in his resignation, but the club president, General John Reed Kilpatrick, refused it and insisted that "Boosh," as he was affectionately known, remain at the helm. With that kind of encouragement, Boucher went into the market and acquired three outstanding prospects in right wing Wally Hergesheimer and defensemen Steve Kraftcheck and Hy Buller. Tony Leswick was traded to Detroit for Gaye Stewart and Gus Kyle was acquired from Boston for Pentti Lund.

These were good deals, but not quite enough to lift the Rangers into the playoffs. Once again they finished fifth. A year later they dropped to sixth, and by the start of the 1953–54 season Ranger fans wondered when, if ever, they'd see a playoff game again. Far from discouraged, Boucher continued to wheel and deal while building up one of the most formidable farm systems in the NHL. He obtained goalie Johnny Bower from Cleveland and electrifying center Max Bentley from Toronto, although the exciting Bentley was thought to be near the end of the trail.

The 1954–55 season was Boucher's last as manager. By this time he had established the Guelph (Ontario) Biltmores as New York's premiere farm team in the powerful Ontario Hockey Association Junior A

League, and the Biltmores were producing one out-standing youngster after another for the Rangers: Andy Bathgate, Dean Prentice, Ron Murphy, Harry Howell, Lou Fontinato, and Aldo Guidolin, to name a few.

Boucher was under pressure to elevate the young-sters, and many came to the NHL earlier than was prudent. As a result it took longer for them to develop as major-leaguers. Then the club missed the playoffs in March 1954. Boucher was replaced by Muzz Patrick. His coaching choice was Phil Watson, and once again the Rangers began winning—with the very same players Boucher had developed for the team.

Unlike Boucher and Patrick, Watson was a wild man who earned the nickname "Phiery Phil." The gospel according to Watson had it that there was no room for prima donnas on the Rangers. Watson once explained it this way:

"The proper spirit means winning hockey games, or at least trying to win hockey games, every minute. That's the way it has to be with my players. Any time one of them gets the notion there's a greater thrill or something else more important in sports than playing winning hockey, he gets a one-way ticket to the min-ors. My players have an obligation to be living, sleep-ing, eating, drinking, and thinking hockey every min-ute. As a matter of honor, they owe it to one another."

Under Watson the Rangers gained playoff berths from 1956 through 1958. In 1959 they blew a nine-point lead to Toronto with two weeks remaining, fin-ished out of the playoffs, and Watson was fired. He was replaced by Alfie Pike, who did little better, and then Doug Harvey, who, as player-coach, got the team back in the playoffs during the 1961–62 season. But Doug ran into trouble the following year and the Rangers were out in the cold again.

As things turned out, their fortunes were not going to change appreciably until Emile Francis took over as manager in October of 1964. Still, there were many exciting nights in those non-Cup years. And the Rangers had come a long way since those dismal days when World War II had depleted their ranks. These were building years, years the Rangers had used for changing direction, sharpening their skills, and gaining experience. The future looked bright, and these were the years that had provided the sunshine.

6. THE LIGHTER SIDE OF THE BLUESHIRTS

Obviously professional hockey players get their greatest amount of pleasure and enjoyment from winning hockey games, and the Rangers are no exception. But even when they weren't winning, the New York skaters have always managed to have their share of laughs.

I would imagine some of the best stories come out of the Rangers' early days, when hockey was still a fly-by-night operation and the Rangers were suffering through the usual absurdities that accompany a fledgling organization. Unfortunately the number of anecdotes about a pro sports team is in direct proportion to their popularity, and in the twenties the newsmen had a hard enough time explaining the game of hockey to their readers. Who had the time or the inclination to go around collecting funny little locker-room stories for their columns? For this reason many of the early humorous incidents have gone unrecorded.

But there's one story I remember from those early years, which is not so much a funny story as it is an indication of how desperate the early Ranger management was to acquire a loving home for their team.

The game of hockey was not the only thing new to New Yorkers in 1926. So were the Rangers, all of them expatriated French-Canadians. Many of the players could not speak a word of English. In those days New York City was even more of a melting pot than it is today. So naturally these strangers from North-of-the-border raised a good deal of suspicion among the local citizenry. Funny little men in funny uniforms playing a funny game will do it every time. The Rangers management was aware of the problem and knew it had to be solved if ticket sales were to continue to rise. A clever publicist hit upon the solution. Lorne Chabot, a Montreal-born French-Canadian, was the Rangers' goaltender in those days and, except for his dark complexion, he looked like every other Canadian on the team. But that was all this publicist needed. From that day on Lorne Chabot became Lorne Chabotsky and was billed as "the only Jewish goalie in professional hockey." This simple technique of name-changing worked so well that several weeks later Oliver Reinikka, a Finnish import by way of Canada, was christened Ollie Rocco. Needless to say, the Italian citizens of New York flocked to the Garden to see their boy play. Looking back on that story, I have to conclude that New Yorkers were a lot more gullible then than they are now.

This had to be the first of a long line of publicity stunts that have come out of the Rangers' public-relations office. But perhaps no one was more willing to climb to new heights of absurdity for a little publicity for his Rangers than Stan Saplin, who served with the

U.S. Navy in World War II and became the Rangers' press agent after the war.

When Saplin worked for the Rangers the Detroit Red Wings had a skater named Fern Gauthier who had once been a prolific scorer but who had fallen into a dreadful slump. A Detroit writer had said that Gauthier couldn't put the puck into the ocean even if he was standing at the end of a pier.

Saplin heard about the allegation and realized that there are no known oceans near Detroit, but there is the Atlantic Ocean off New York City. He contacted the Red Wings and asked their front office if they'd mind letting Gauthier in on a publicity stunt.

The good-natured Detroiters agreed, and a few weeks later, when the Red Wings came to New York, Saplin got together with Gauthier and explained his project. Saplin, Gauthier, a couple of other Detroit players, and a photographer would take the subway down to the tip of Manhattan Island. They would take a pail full of hockey pucks and a stick. With the pucks sitting at the edge of the pier, Gauthier would then prove that he *could* shoot the puck into the ocean.

When the group arrived at the appointed spot, a number of New Yorkers looked on in amazement at a young man shooting round black disks in the direction of the water. There is photographic proof that Gauthier did get the pucks into the ocean, although rumor has it that he missed on his first two tries.

One of the most bizarre episodes during the Saplin era involved Tony Leswick, the short, hard-checking forward who specialized in troublemaking. At lunch one afternoon Leswick, teammate Don Raleigh, and Raleigh's brother, Jack, were sitting at a table in a cafeteria across from the Garden discussing the developments of the previous evening. Their conversation dealt with the banging of skulls on the ice, with frequent threats such as "I'll get him!"

"This went on for a while," said Leswick. "All of a sudden we heard somebody yell at us, 'Stand up!' You knew from the tone of the voice that he wasn't kidding. We jumped up and saw that there were three men, one behind each of us.

"The first thing, they frisked us. Then I saw that the fellow covering me had a gun. Brother, was I scared! They began to throw questions at us. I couldn't figure the thing out. First I thought it was a holdup. But as they kept firing questions at us I realized they thought *we* were holdup men. They were detectives.

"You would never think it possible, but a guy who'd been sitting near us had heard us talking and it sounded like underworld language to him. He phoned the police station. 'Ice' was interpreted as jewelry, 'stick' meant stickup, and so on.

"We convinced them finally that we were hockey players. Later when we all went over to the Garden, I told the detective who had been covering me that for a minute I had been thinking of making a break. I asked him what he would have done about it. He said he would have shot me. I didn't get over that for weeks."

Of course the Rangers have not been without their

share of comics, cut-ups, and aspiring stand-up comedians. The prime source of humor, from 1935 through 1943, was none other than Walter, "Babe," Pratt, the rather large defenseman from Manitoba who enjoyed the good life and the grape. Pratt always was good for a laugh, whether he was on the giving or receiving end of a joke, and the Rangers scene was that much richer for the Babe being a part of it.

When Babe reported to training camp in September 1940 he was full of ginger, and he didn't slow down as the Rangers embarked on their usual exhibition tour. One night he checked into the team's Pullman car at 3 a.m., only to discover that Lester was waiting up for him. "Babe," said Patrick, "I'm fining you $1,000. But if you don't take another drink for the rest of the campaign, I'll refund your money at the end of the season."

Pratt went on the wagon and the Rangers went on a long, long losing streak. Patrick was worried and, one day, suggested to Babe that maybe a drink wouldn't hurt after all. "No, no," said Pratt, "my word is my bond."

Word of the Patrick–Pratt meeting leaked to the players. They figured that if Babe didn't get off the wagon the club would really be in trouble. They told Pratt they would chip in and raise $1,000 if only he would have an occasional drink or two. But Pratt was adamant. The Rangers wound up in fourth place and were knocked right out of the playoffs by Detroit. "There's a moral to that story," Pratt said years later, "but I've been trying for thirty years and still haven't been able to figure it out."

The Babe and Lester didn't always get along, especially when money was the subject. According to Pratt, Patrick wasn't tight with money, "he was adjacent to it!" Lester finally traded Babe to Toronto in 1942, and to Pratt's astonishment he was paid more by the Leafs than Lester ever paid him. As a result he began to play even better. When Lester found out about Pratt's good fortune, he asked Babe about it. "Lester," Pratt explained, "now I'm being paid enough to eat on. I'm finally getting the wrinkles out of my belly!"

Conn Smythe took over where Lester had left off, but Babe never stopped being Babe, always good for the laughs. Meantime the Rangers had plenty of fun without him. Lynn Patrick likes to tell the story about a trick Lester used when the Rangers were protecting a lead in the late stages of a game.

"The pucks used in a game," said Lynn, "are frozen to make them stay flat on the ice. Lester always kept a warm puck in his pocket. If the Rangers were a goal ahead in the late stages of a game in Madison Square Garden, out would go the warm puck. The thing would hop like a wild rabbit and the opposing team always had trouble controlling it. The Rangers protected quite a few leads that way."

Occasionally old Rangers would get together in the minors, where many of them settled to become coaches. Bun Cook was one of them. He ended up in Cleveland, coaching Jim Hendy's Barons of the American League at a time when Babe Pratt was skating out his career with the Hershey Bears.

Once Cleveland was demolishing Pratt's Hershey

sextet, 9–0. Late in the game Babe, who was well on in his hockey years, skated past the Barons' bench. His old pal, Cook, looked up at the scoreboard and shouted down to Pratt, "It's 9–0, Babe. What are you going to do about it."

"Nothing to it," Babe shot back. "A touchdown and a field goal."

Going back a couple of decades brings to mind the years the Rangers were quite devout and, on occasion, would drop in at St. Malachy's Chapel on 49th Street before a home game. Chuck Rayner tended goal for the Rangers in those days. Chuck was not a religious fanatic, but on this particular day he was about to face the rugged Bruins and he figured a few pre-game words with the Almighty certainly couldn't hurt anything.

A couple of hours later Chuck showed up in the dressing room with his brows furrowed and a look of concern on his face. The puck would hit the ice in less than an hour and the Rangers couldn't afford to have a goalie with anything on his mind other than blocking that little black disk. Naturally Chuck's teammates asked him what was wrong.

"Get ready for a hell of a hockey game," Chuck replied. "I just came from St. Malachy's and the Boston goalie was in there too."

Some of the funnier moments for the Rangers came during games, right in the heat of battle. More often than not, the humor of such episodes did not become apparent until after the game, when the players had a chance to reflect. Phil Watson told me a story, and he swears that at the time it happened his motives were dictated solely by common sense. Watson probably had more "disagreements" in his career than any player in Ranger history. But in the greatest Garden free-for-all of them all, March 16, 1947, vs. Montreal, "Phiery Phil" was the only noncombatant. How come? Phil put it this way:

"I remembered the story about Frank Boucher and Dit Clapper. Boucher, during a fight between Rangers and Bruins, told Dit, 'What's the use of getting all tangled up? Let's you and me stand on the side and watch this one.' Which is exactly what they did.

"So I grabbed hold of George Allen of the Canadiens and convinced him to sit this one out. While the fighting was going on we just stood by and watched. You know, it was fun."

No player receives as much physical abuse as a goaltender, and no goaltender in Ranger history was so bombarded by rubber as Steve Buzinski, a youthful wartime replacement in 1942–43. It's been said that Steve had a sunburn on his neck caused by the perennial glow of the red goal light behind him.

Despite the fact that his average (6.11)' was abominable, Steve had a delightful way about him and even fancied himself a pretty fair goalie. Asked how it felt to stop big-league shots after jumping straight from the Swift Current (Saskatchewan) Intermediates, Buzinski replied, "Same as back home. It's easy as pickin' cherries off a tree." Shortly after that deathless remark Steve stopped a high backhander and nonchalantly tossed the puck to the side of the net. Unfortunately it was the wrong side, the red light pointing out his error to thousands of exasperated fans.

A living legend among hockey people is Vernon, "Jakie," Forbes, who later became a crockery salesman. They say he played for more pro teams than any goalie in captivity.

"I had to quit hockey," Jake explained. "I played with and against so many players I couldn't tell who was on my side anymore."

Ex-Ranger backliner Bill Gadsby tells one that happened a few years back when he was with Chicago. Seems the Hawks and Montreal were playing a Stanley Cup semifinal in Chicago and the fans were in a gay mood.

In the second period Butch Bouchard of Montreal was skating past the boards when suddenly a fan tossed a jigger of whiskey in his face. Enraged, Butch yelled for the referee, Red Storey, to eject the fan. But Storey couldn't hear Butch above the din of the crowd. Again Butch squealed. Storey shouted back that he couldn't hear a thing Butch was saying.

"Well, if you can't hear me," said Bouchard, skating up to Storey's face, "smell me."

Lester Patrick, whom I have already mentioned in several stories, remembers the time during his coaching days when Colonel John Hammond, then president of the Rangers, called him into his office. Hammond, a tight man with the dollar, wanted to buy the Boston Bruins' Eddie Shore, who was already established as an NHL superstar. All Hammond was willing to offer for Shore was one of his second-stringers, a guy named Myles Lane, and five thousand dollars in cash. Patrick knew the Boston owner, Charles Adams, and told the Colonel on the spot that Adams would laugh in his face. But Hammond would not listen to reason and made the offer anyway. Several weeks later Colonel Hammond showed Patrick the wire he had received from Mr. Adams. It read: YOU ARE SO MANY MYLES FROM SHORE, YOU NEED A LIFE PRE-SERVER.

One of the strangest—and funniest—events in Rangers History involved a black bottle and a hockey writer named Jim Burchard who covered the Rangers for many years for the *New York World-Telegram*.

The episode took place during a Blueshirt slump which seemed to be going on and on. Those were the days when Gene Leone operated Mamma Leone's Restaurant near the old Garden. Gene was a red-hot Rangers fan as well as an excellent restaurateur.

Worried about the Rangers' losing streak, Leone decided that something had to be done to help the team. He pored over the ingredients in his kitchen, and suddenly an idea hit him. He'd distill some delectable juices, mix them with vintage wine, and produce a wonderful winning tonic for his Rangers.

Just before Christmas Leone perfected his formula and poured it into a large black container about three times the size of a normal whiskey bottle. With appropriate fuss and fanfare "Leone's Magic Elixir" was carried into the Ranger dressing room, where such heroes as Bones Raleigh, Pentti Lund, Frankie Eddolls, Neil Colville, and Zellio Toppazzini quaffed the brew.

To say the results were amazing would be an understatement. They were hallucinatory. The Rangers began to win and win. By early January they had lost only two of their past eleven games. But observers insisted the real test would come when the Blueshirts visited Toronto, where they had gone ages without a victory.

Now the fun started. Leone demanded that the magic elixir—the formula was so secret he wouldn't even trust it to paper—be prepared at the last possible moment. This was done on Saturday afternoon. When the elixir was ready, he turned it over to Jim Burchard, who boarded a plane for Toronto. The idea was for Jim to arrive just before game time and then present the potion.

Wearing his traditional black hat with big brim turned down on each side, Burchard boarded the plane carrying a hermetically sealed bag containing the elixir in a black bottle, surrounded by three hot-water bottles. A skull and crossbones adorned the black carrying case.

Unknown to the Ranger strategists, the Maple Leaf organization was arranging for the Canadian customs agent to seize the black bottle at Toronto Airport, denying its use to the New Yorkers. "Naturally," wrote Al Nickleson in the *Globe and Mail,* "the Leafs had been hoping the flagon would have been seized by customs when Burchard couldn't explain its contents."

But a *Globe* photographer named Harold Robinson saved the Rangers, said Nickleson, "by undermining the customs officer with stale jokes and Christmas cigars so that Burchard had no trouble slipping by." Then Robinson pushed Burchard into his car and set several Ontario speed records driving to Maple Leaf Gardens, arriving just in time for quaffing.

Naturally Burchard forgot a corkscrew, so he had

to push the cork down into the bottle in the manner of an impatient rum connoisseur. The Rangers, who actually detested the vile stuff, had their brief sips—some just gargled, and spat it out—then returned the bottle to Burchard.

"When the cork stops disintegrating," explained Burchard as he poured what the Rangers couldn't drink down the sink, "we know that the stuff has lost its power. Why look at that! Here comes a mouse up the drain waving a white flag."

The Rangers, who enjoyed the jape more than the elixir itself, had their laughs and then went out on the ice and performed like supermen. Within seven minutes of the first period they scored three goals, and then coasted to a 4–2 win.

This caused a sensation. "CAMERAMAN LUGS FLAGITIOUS FLAGON," screamed a headline in the *Globe and Mail*. "RANGERS NEW AID SCORNED BY LEAFS," the Toronto *Telegram* roared. Leone said he'd bottle the stuff and sell it commercially, while players and scientists speculated on its contents.

"It tasted like the Atlantic Ocean," said photographer Robinson. "I think it's hot broth," said Leafs coach Joe Primeau. The Rangers had other thoughts that are not fit for these pages, but the idea was appropriately conveyed by Toronto writer Bob Hesketh, who tasted the stuff. "It was a creamy liquid," said Hesketh, "that smelled just like water doesn't."

Occasionally Leone would be distracted by business and forget to distill the potion. When the Rangers lost to Detroit, Burchard explained, "The Leone brew wasn't on deck. Without it the Rangers were under a psychological handicap."

An sos was dispatched to Leone, who quickly prepared more of the liquid, and the Rangers whipped Toronto, 2–1, the next night.

And so it went. Two weeks later Burchard arrived in Toronto without the bottle and the paper screamed. They attributed the Ranger loss that night to the missing elixir. But Leone soon produced more, and the Rangers remained contenders until late in the season, when they faded into fifth.

It was a memorable year, and not only because of Leone, Burchard, and the black bottle. It was the year a tiny goalie made his debut as a Ranger. He played several games, then drifted away. Unlike the black bottle, he eventually returned to become the Blueshirts' latter-day elixir.

That man was Emile Francis.

7. ENTER EMILE FRANCIS

The Rangers were going nowhere fast during the years prior to Emile Francis' appointment as general manager on October 30, 1964. In the six previous seasons the Rangers had gained a playoff berth but once —during that very special season when defense great Doug Harvey both coached and played for the New Yorkers.

In the season preceding Emile's appointment the Rangers were a dismal fifth, with only twenty-two wins against thirty-eight losses and ten ties. It was obvious that a monumental rebuilding job had to be done, and it was begun by manager Murray, "Muzz," Patrick, who had imported Francis as his assistant during the 1963–64 season.

Working as a unit, the Patrick-Francis tandem pulled off a mammoth trade in February 1964 when they dealt Andy Bathgate and Don McKenney to Toronto for Rod Seiling, Bob Nevin, Arnie Brown, Dick Duff, and Bill Collins. I, for one, was very unhappy about the trade because Bathgate had been one of my favorite Rangers—a classy hockey player and a classy guy.

Looking at it realistically, however, I had to admit that Bathgate and McKenney were over the hill and the Rangers would be receiving a number of gifted young players who would be around the NHL for years and years after both Bathgate and McKenney retired.

The problem for Patrick was that the younger players he had obtained needed time to develop and, unfortunately for him, time was running out. It had been decided by the Garden brass to move Patrick into a vice-presidency and let Francis manage the club.

If Emile had any doubts about what had to be done, he merely had to recall an episode that occurred after he came to New York as Patrick's assistant. There was trouble in Kitchener, Ontario, where the Rangers were operating a developmental team. The manager of the Kitchener junior club phoned Francis to tell him that the kids there needed new uniforms; the ones they were wearing were threadbare.

"Sure," said Emile, "I'll send you up a batch of our Rangers' uniforms. They're used, but they're still in good shape."

The Kitchener manager was enthusiastic until the uniforms arrived. Immediately he got on the phone to Francis. "Sorry," he said, "but those uniforms are too small."

That was the tip-off. Emile knew that he had to find bigger, more muscular players if the Rangers were going to climb out of the NHL doldrums. Finding big ones was easy; finding good ones was another story. But Francis applied himself to the task, and soon the new faces arrived. He traded Camille Henry, Don Johns, Wally Chevrier, and Bill Taylor to the Chicago Black Hawks for husky Wayne Hillman and Doug Robinson, as well as John Brenneman, a small but fleet young forward.

He dealt John McKenzie, who was doing nothing for the Rangers, to Boston for effervescent Reg Fleming, and obtained Orland Kurtenbach, a tall center and one of the best fighters in the league, from the Toronto Maple Leafs. Even in those early years players who had had just a taste of the Francis system left raving about the new manager.

"He's the finest man I've met in hockey," said McKenzie after he had been traded to the Bruins. "Maybe I didn't cut the mustard in New York, but it was no fault of Emile's. He's a helluva guy."

Meanwhile Rangers fans were getting impatient. Francis wasn't. He understood that patience was important and he studied the club with Argus eyes to determine where improvements could be made. One area was coaching. Francis had inherited Red Sullivan as the club's bench boss when he took over. Sullivan stayed on for more than a year after Emile's appointment, and then Francis decided it was time for a change. On December 5, 1965, Sullivan was fired and on December 6, 1965, Francis became coach as well as manager.

"It'll take two years before we reach the playoffs," he said. His first full year was 1965–66. The club finished dead last. The next season, as predicted, the Rangers had climbed to fourth. They would never miss the playoffs again under Francis.

"One deal more than any other helped move us up," Francis told me. "That was the one that brought Eddie Giacomin to New York. I had to give up four players (Aldo Guidolin, Jim Mikol, Sandy McGregor, and Marcel Paille) to get him, but it was worth it."

I wasn't so sure about it at first, and neither were the Ranger fans. Giacomin had originally been signed as an understudy for Jacques Plante for the 1965–66 season, but when Plante "retired" during the summer of 1965, Giacomin automatically became the first-string goalie.

Eddie had his problems at first, but so did the entire team for that matter—right down to the Rangers' movie projector. One day, while the players were watching films of a game they had played the night before, the projector caught fire and blew up.

To make the playoffs, Francis needed a leader. He took a gamble and signed right wing Bernie, "Boom Boom," Geoffrion, who had been coaching in Quebec. A lot of people figured that signing the Boomer was nothing more than a publicity stunt, but Geoffrion had other ideas. His dressing-room monologues lifted the Rangers' spirits, and his inspirational efforts on the ice helped convert Rod Gilbert into a star player. While he was at it he dropped in more than his share of goals.

Francis' faith was rewarded in other ways. He remembered defenseman Rod Seiling when others had forgotten him. He reclaimed Rod in the draft, and watched him blossom into one of the NHL's steadiest and cleanest defensemen.

Another who benefitted under Francis's guidance was defenseman Arnie Brown. Nobody has put it better than Brown on the day he told me how Francis had changed the image of the Rangers: "Emile injected warmth and feeling," said Arnie. "He made you feel as if you are playing for a real club. He's the greatest."

Brown didn't stay in New York forever. Like others, he was traded. Red Berenson, from whom so much had been expected and so little delivered, also was sent packing. In time Berenson was traded to St. Louis, but he never put Francis down for the move. "I wasn't crazy about the way I played," said Berenson, "but that was no reflection on Emile. I've got nothing but good things to say about him. Maybe this is why: When he traded me, he didn't say a word about the deal until he personally got in touch with me. And that wasn't easy. I was out of the house for quite some time and he couldn't reach me. A lot of other managers wouldn't have been as sensitive about it as Emile. It's a little thing but it's the kind of thing a player appreciates."

Sometimes the praise for Francis came from the most unlikely places; even from Alan Eagleson, executive director of the NHL Players' Association and a man who, over the years, had battled fiercely with most coaches and managers. In February 1973 Eagleson offered a man-by-man review of the coaches and managers in the league. He was brutally harsh with some, and not so pleasant with others ("Vancouver has a lot of problems because Vic Stasiuk has a lot of problems"), but when it came to Francis, Eagleson glowed.

"Emile has the complete relationship with his players," said Eagleson. "And this is reflected in their play. One admirable thing about Francis: he calls his young players into his office and he tells them that if they don't make his team, he will get them a job somewhere else. And he has done this with many players, such as Syl Apps, Jr., Mike Murphy, Jack Egers, Steve Durbano, Mike Robitaille, and Pierre Jarry."

What many fans don't realize is that Francis has been able to be so complete a manager and coach because he has been doing this work for most of his life. He broke in as a semipro baseball manager in his twenties, playing in a strong Western Canadian League against players who eventually made it to the majors. Another thing many spectators don't know is that Francis helped introduce the goaltender's trapper glove to hockey as a direct result of his baseball experiences. He once told me about it:

"When I first started playing goal," Francis said, "I had a lot of trouble with the gloves we wore then (the mid-forties). To tell you the truth, my hands are still a bit mushy from catching with the old gloves. I felt there had to be a way of improving the goaltender's equipment. So I decided to bring something in from baseball—the first-baseman's mitt.

"I wore it one night in Detroit when King Clancy was refereeing. Jack Adams was manager of the Red Wings in those days and he was a crusty old guy. He called over to Clancy and protested, although he said he would tolerate it for that one night until he could check the rules to see if it was legal." As things turned out, there was nothing illegal about the trapper, and it soon became a part of the goaltender's standard equipment.

Emile was playing goal in New York long before I started broadcasting. He actually played at Madison Square Garden during the 1942–43 season with the Philadelphia Falcons of the Eastern League, although he was Detroit Red Wings property. A year later he played for the Washington Lions in the Eastern League for fifty dollars a week. From Washington he enlisted in the Canadian Army until the end of World War II, when he signed with Moose Jaw, Saskatchewan, and became the property of the Chicago Black Hawks. In 1946–47 he played nineteen games with the Black Hawks, and a year later became the regular Chicago goalie. Eventually he made his way to the Rangers system, but never played regularly again in the NHL.

The fact that Emile never was a big-league star is irrelevant to his success as a manager. What matters is that he never stopped studying and he never gave up. He was a goaltender for nineteen seasons with twelve different teams. As a big-leaguer with Chicago and New York, he played in only ninety-five games, but he proved himself a hard-nosed goalie.

Once, while goaltending for New Haven in the American League, he dislocated a shoulder, but played the rest of the game with a harness. Because he couldn't get his arm up to protect his face, he lost five teeth and suffered a split nose when a shot struck him. Remarkably he finished the game. Only after his teeth were broken did the trainer persuade him to loosen the harness.

His toughness was translated to the Rangers' style of play. The club finished second to the Montreal Canadiens during the 1967–68 season and gained a playoff berth in each of the seasons thereafter. The toughness took on many forms. Some were training rules. Others were rules about life styles which Emile believed were important in molding a winner. Always, he was thinking.

During the 1973 playoff against the Bruins, Francis moved the Rangers out of New York City and holed them up in Fitchburg, Massachusetts. With the players' privacy insured, he filled their time with game films and held drills twice a day.

By contrast, the Bruins were treating the upcoming series with an almost militant casualness. The Rangers won the series in five games, and some players insist that Francis' strategy was the reason. "I didn't think going to Fitchburg was all that important at first," said left wing Steve Vickers. "But the more I thought about it, the more I was convinced that going there was the reason why we beat Boston so easily. We'd been playing bad hockey for a while. Emile took us away to bring us back together again as a team. It worked."

Brad Park has said that he respects Francis as much as any man he's met in hockey and appreciates his way with the players. "The Cat," said Park, "is a fascinating man. After a workout he'll bring the team together to examine the mistakes we've made, but he'll never mention a specific player's name. Naturally, though, everybody knows exactly who's being discussed and makes no bones about it."

Emile is also a bug for statistics, another element of his intense study of the game, and has several theories about what makes a winner. Once, last season, he told me one of his ideas. "Any time our defensemen take ten to fourteen shots a game," said Francis, "it means we're controlling the puck and should win."

Defenseman Jim Neilson elaborated. "According to Emile's plan," said Neilson, "our defensemen function like backcourtmen in basketball. If one of our forwards can't take the shot or make the pass inside, he gets the puck back to the blue line and we try to set up the play all over again. When the system is working, it means we keep the puck in the other team's end a lot longer, but it also means the defensemen are getting a lot more shots."

Among NHL coaches and managers Francis had the best record of leading a club into the playoffs—seven out of the last seven years. But on June 4, 1973, Francis decided that the dual job of managing *and* coaching was too much for one man in a 16-team NHL. Larry Popein, a member of the Rangers' organization for 21 of his 22 years in pro hockey, signed a two-year contract to coach the Rangers. Still, the Francis philosophy will prevail. Overseeing Popein's arrival were Madison Square Garden chairman Irving Mitchell Felt and Rangers' president Bill Jennings, who quietly had piloted the Rangers into their Golden Age along with Francis.

"You have to sacrifice," he told me. "I played goal for fourteen years and I sacrificed. By hard work— good, honest toil—we'll reach our goal."

I have to go along with Manager Francis. Every year the Rangers play with a little more polish, a little more poise. Had it not been for the injury epidemic, 1972–73 might have been their season. Maybe this season will produce that "goal" Emile has been reaching for. Let's take a look at some of the players that could make it happen.

8. BRAD PARK, THE CORNERSTONE

I was there when the Brad Park miracle happened. It was September 1968 and I was covering the Rangers' training camp in Kitchener, Ontario. Bernie, "Boom Boom," Geoffrion had just taken over as coach. Emile Francis had chosen to confine himself to the manager's duties.

My reasons for being at the training camp weren't limited to reporting alone. I had a personal interest, too, because my kid brother, Al, was there trying out as a goaltender.

It was an exciting camp. But the excitement was tainted with tragedy. On the very first day of workouts Geoffrion had the minor-leaguers going through the training paces, consisting mostly of light skates and occasional end-to-end rushes. The weather was balmy, warm enough to go swimming, and not very conducive to hockey.

The practice had barely begun when one of the players fell to his knees and then keeled over completely on the ice. His name was Wayne Larkin and he had played good hockey in the minors for a number of years. This was considered his last real chance to make it in the NHL.

For a split-second the players thought it was some kind of gag. After all, the opening day of training camp usually isn't taken all that seriously and loosening up with some humor is all part of the routine. But as Larkin's face turned ashen white it became clear that this was no joke.

Geoffrion was the first to sense something unusual and he rushed over to Larkin. "I was afraid he might have had a heart attack," the Boomer told me later in his motel room. Geoffrion tried mouth-to-mouth resuscitation, but Larkin didn't respond. An emergency call was put in to the Kitchener hospital. In the meantime a doctor who happened to be on the scene pounded Larkin's chest to revive his heartbeat—but to no avail. By the time the ambulance arrived and the stricken skater was removed to the hospital, it had become apparent that he was dead. Before the first afternoon of the first day of training camp that September, one very fine professional hockey player was dead.

I had never seen anything like that before, have never experienced an athletic tragedy like that since— and I hope I never do. The incident cast a pall over the entire camp, and the players all went back to the Holiday Inn Motel in Kitchener to await notice of when the workouts would resume. Once the impact of the tragedy had subsided I went into Geoffrion's room and discussed his team's prospects for the 1968–69 season.

The Boomer, who had been stunned by the Larkin

incident, took his mind off the tragedy with a review of his lineup. He was solid in goal with Eddie Giacomin and Gilles Villemure. Up front the club was oozing with talent—Jean Ratelle, Vic Hadfield, Rod Gilbert, Dave Balon, Bob Nevin, and Orland Kurtenbach, to name a few. The defense looked equally solid, anchored by Harry Howell, Jim Neilson, Rod Seiling, and Arnie Brown.

What excited Geoffrion more than anything was the surplus of good young hockey players in camp and the challenge of finding places for them in the lineup. Two players emerged as virtual sure bets to crack the big lineup. Walter Tkaczuk, a muscular center from South Porcupine, Ontario, had drawn raves from the Rangers scouts, particularly Steve Brklacich. The other was defenseman Al Hamilton, who had been up to the Rangers on previous occasions for the proverbial "cup of coffee," but was believed capable of sticking with the big team this time around.

In fact Hamilton was given the edge over Tkaczuk by virtue of his experience and the fact that his time was due. It was as simple as that. True, Geoffrion talked about the others. He mentioned a hard-nosed right wing named Bill Fairbairn and he talked about a couple of kid defensemen right out of junior hockey. One of them was Mike Robitaille, who had played for the Rangers' farm team, in a strong Junior A League.

If there was anybody who could bump Hamilton off the varsity, it would be young Robitaille. He was husky and smart and had a mean slapshot. He had scored twenty goals and fifty-one assists for Kitchener, which accounted, in part, for his mountain of positive press clippings. Right off the bat he looked like a winner.

"There's another kid here who's supposed to be pretty good," said Geoffrion. "His name is Park, but I don't know too much about him. We'll have to wait and see."

Nobody knew too much about Park because there really wasn't much to know. Certainly none of the writers knew about him, nor did I or any of the other members of the radio-television contingent. Nothing was said about him by the Rangers publicity department because nobody knew anything about this young man who looked like a high school sophomore.

Just about the only ones who *did* know anything about Brad Park were Brad Park and his mother and father. By no small coincidence the three of them were sitting in the stands at Kitchener Memorial Gardens the day training camp began. I remember thinking at the time this kid isn't here to make the Rangers but to watch his idols go through some scrimmages.

Who ever heard of a professional hockey player showing up for a tryout with his mother and father? This seemed a bit much to me and not the stuff I expected from an NHL camp.

But shortly thereafter I ran into Carl Martin, hockey writer for the *Hudson Dispatch*. "You won't believe this," said Martin, "but I just talked to a twenty-year-old kid who thinks he's good enough to beat out Al Hamilton as the fifth defenseman. What's more, he even thinks he's good enough to be a regular."

I assumed that Martin was talking about Mike Robitaille, a player that I had been told was known for occasional bursts of brashness. "No," Martin went on, "it's not Robitaille. The kid's name is Park—Brad Park—and I had a long talk with him and his father. After listening to them, I'm almost inclined to believe them."

We both had a good chuckle. After all, the fifth defense spot was signed, sealed, and delivered to Hamilton. We knew that. The other media people knew that. And, we believed, so did the Rangers brass. But based on what Martin had told me, I decided to make a point of watching this young hot dog.

For the next three days I watched Park carefully and, I have to admit, certain aspects of his repertoire impressed me. His slapshot from the point was crisp, low, and on target. He skated with strong strides and, more important, with confidence. And in the brisk body-to-body confrontations with the seasoned pros, he not only held his own but deposited many a veteran on his backside with the same kind of submarine check that was made famous in another era by the late Bill Barilko of the Toronto Maple Leafs. Later I learned that Bob Park, Brad's dad, had been an amateur hockey coach in Toronto and had been friendly with Barilko in 1951. That was the year that Barilko won the Cup with a sudden-death goal against the Montreal Canadiens in the fifth game of the finals. Park Sr. also was chummy with Max Bentley, one of the greatest stickhandlers of all time, and it appeared that some of Bentley's stick magic had become a part of young Brad's movements. Against my better judgment I became a Brad Park fan in less than a week.

I say "better judgment" because it is never wise for

a broadcaster to have personal feelings about any player, rookie *or* veteran. By the same token, it must be remembered that we are human and it was perfectly natural to root for this pleasantly brash kid to make the team—although I was still certain that he was several dreams away from the varsity.

After two weeks of exhibition games I began to notice an interesting development among members of the media. There seemed to be a grass-roots movement in support of Park. Suddenly his name no longer inspired looks of amazement or the "Who's he?" kind of response. In fact when talk about the Rangers defense surfaced, Park's name was now appearing ahead of Robitaille's and not far behind Hamilton's.

The real turning point for Park came on Madison Square Garden ice. Francis had scheduled an exhibition game against the Montreal Canadiens and Park was listed as one of the starters. Robitaille, by this time, was out of the picture and the battle for the fifth defense job was now between Park and Hamilton.

On the basis of that game alone, Hamilton was a goner. Within two periods Brad had captured the imagination of the Garden crowd, a crowd that has always had a nose for the spectacular. The clincher came when Park stopped a Montreal attack and counterattacked with Rod Gilbert on his flank. Jacques Laperriere, one of the NHL's best defensemen, was trying to cover the two-on-one break when Park sent a pass to Gilbert. Both Brad and Laperriere expected Gilbert to shoot, but Rod fooled everybody and dropped the puck right back to Park's stick. He was thirty feet from the net, so he wound up and sent the puck on a bee-line into the upper left corner of the net. Park had it made with the Rangers. So he thought. So I thought and so the newspapermen thought.

Francis had other ideas. For one thing, he had a commitment to Hamilton, at least to give him one more complete shot at the big-time. For another, he had a commitment to Park's future. It didn't make sense to elevate Brad at a critical time in his hockey-learning process and then just sit him on the bench where he could become jaded and depressed.

"I had to send Brad to the minors," said Francis, "for everybody's benefit."

With the promise that he would be the first defenseman recalled, Park was sent to Buffalo, then a Rangers' farm team in the American League. It was a very bitter pill for the kid because he knew he had major-league skills.

As things turned out, Brad Park had the guts to swallow his pride, and it wasn't very long before he was back in the big-time to stay. At the time he was comforted by the fact that his buddy, Walt Tkaczuk, also was dispatched to Buffalo. Tkaczuk was recalled after five games. Twelve games later Park got the call from Francis. He was now a Ranger, never to ride another minor-league bench in his life.

His joy was short-lived. After he had fit himself in snugly with the big club, helping them win a few games, the Rangers lost their winning touch. Defeat was piled on defeat and the New Yorkers plummeted to the ground floor.

Quite naturally coach Geoffrion went to his veterans for help. Both Park and Tkaczuk were benched and replaced by seasoned skaters. The move hurt the kids and, as luck would have it, hurt the team as well. It was a perplexing situation from every angle. Geoffrion's health had deteriorated along with the club's standing, and it became difficult to separate one from the other. One Friday night in late January, after a game in Oakland, the Boomer became so ill he had to be hospitalized. Francis replaced him and stayed behind the bench for the rest of the season. Park and Tkaczuk once more became regulars, and the two justified their assignments.

In fifty-four games as a rookie Brad scored three goals and twenty-three assists for twenty-six points. He added two more assists in the four playoff games. Brad Park was no longer an unknown with the look of a high school sophomore. He had developed into a confident young professional, and when training camp opened the next year, he was enroute to his first of several All-Star seasons.

The arrival of Park meant the departure of Hamilton. It also meant the beginning of the inevitable comparisons to Bobby Orr. I, for one, would not suggest that Brad is as good a total player as Orr, but I would not shrink from a comparison of the two.

First of all, one must bear in mind that Orr has been in the NHL a lot longer than Park. In Brad's rookie season, Bobby was already into his third full major-league campaign. He had absorbed a tremendous amount of knowledge while Park was still playing with the juniors. Look at the 1971–72 season. By then Brad had four full years under his belt and, like

Orr, was unequivocally an All-Star. In that year Park broke one Rangers record after another. His twenty-four goals was a club record for defensemen, as were his forty-nine assists and seventy-three total points. On December 12, 1971, he became the first Rangers defenseman to score the hat trick, an accomplishment he duplicated on February 12, 1972.

And all things considered, Brad is more of a defensive defenseman than Orr. Park uses the submarine bodycheck to greater advantage and is caught up ice less frequently. Bobby, on the other hand, is unquestionably a better skater and a better offensive threat. And, of course, Orr has stood the test of time longer than Park. What is most relevant, however, is the value of each to his team. Granted, the Bruins without Orr are like baby cubs. But the Rangers without Park? Look at the statistics. In one stretch of the 1972–73 season the Rangers won twenty-nine games, lost seven, and tied three with Park *in* the lineup. When he was sidelined they won twelve, lost nine, and tied three. "Park gives the Rangers momentum," said one New York hockey analyst. "With him they are a special team."

Brad resembles more than any of the modern defensemen the great Doug Harvey of the Montreal Canadiens—and later the Rangers and St. Louis Blues —on defense. Harvey was cool and calculating. He had that special magnetic touch with the puck: able to diddle and daddle with it at his skates, able to speed up ice like a locomotive and then suddenly bring the pace down to one mile an hour. So it is with Park. He is the commanding general of the Rangers' attack *and* defense.

When the enemy assault spills over the blue line, Brad's tenacious stick is there to disrupt the attack. But he doesn't stop there. Inevitably he will relieve the enemy of the puck and, just as important, set it in motion for one of his attacking teammates. "As the centerman," Jean Ratelle once said, "I'm the key to the offense, but first I have to get the puck. Brad gets me the puck."

Brad became a marked man in the Boston Garden in 1971–72 because of certain unpleasant observations he made about the Bruins in his book, *Play the Man*. As a result, he became a sitting duck for the angry Boston skaters and their fans.

Lesser types might have charged they had been misquoted. Brad never did. He stuck by his statements without equivocating. "I wanted to write an honest hockey book," he said. "I think I did. I just put down the way I felt after certain games. I wasn't looking for any love from Boston fans."

Bruins heavyweights Wayne Cashman, Ken Hodge, and Ted Green laid the lumber on Park's broad back that season. He took on all comers. On several occasions a second Bruin player had to come to the rescue of his beaten teammate as Brad pummeled his hapless adversary.

"I love to fight," Brad told an interviewer during the 1972–73 season. Sure he does, but I'm convinced that he fights only when he believes he can help his team. Given the choice between fighting and playing his steady, commanding game, Brad will choose the latter.

The similarity between Park and Orr extends still further. Like the Bruins superman, Brad has suffered knee problems ever since his days as a junior with the Toronto Marlboros. Early in the 1972–73 season it appeared that Orr had not fully recovered from his delicate knee operation of the previous summer and was playing at less than his full capacity. I recall Brad's sensitive understanding of his opponent's condition. "It's a shame to see a guy who means so much to his team get hurt. But in this game you never know. One day everything's going great; the next day, bang, you get hurt and can't play."

Brad spoke from experience. Unfortunately he was also being prophetic. On November 15, 1972, defenseman Ed Van Impe of the Philadelphia Flyers crashed into Park a split-second after Brad had delivered a hard shot on goal. Van Impe's check had once again damaged Brad's knee. Brad missed twenty-six of the team's seventy-eight games that season.

It could be said that Van Impe's body block cost the Rangers first place and the Prince of Wales Trophy. I would have understood if Brad had been bitter about Van Impe's blast. But he just isn't that way. "He's more like a Huckleberry Finn on skates," said Stan Isaacs, sports editor of *Newsday,* the Long Island daily. And I agree. While recuperating in the hospital, Brad carefully analyzed Van Impe's move with professional admiration.

"I saw Van Impe coming at me as I shot. I was falling to my left, so I really didn't think he'd get to me. After I shot and followed through, my weight was on the right foot. He drove at me from the side. He came in low. His shoulder caught my leg and I went down. You don't see many defensemen dive at a guy from the side, but it was a clean hit."

With Park playing in only fifty-two games, the Rangers finished third. Orr played sixty-three games for the Bruins and Boston finished second. Facing each other in the opening round of the Stanley Cup playoffs, Brad came off the winner, four games to one.

What will happen in the seasons to come depends, in part, on how well Brad's knees hold up. *Sport* magazine put it in perspective during the 1972–73 season with this headline:

"WHEN BRAD PARK GETS HURT, EVERY RANGER FEELS THE PAIN."

9. WALT TKACZUK, PERFECTLY INDESTRUCTIBLE

Put a jet engine in a bulldozer, add some dedication and some hockey brains, and you have an idea of what Walter Tkaczuk means to the Rangers and to his opponents. If any hockey player can be defined in terms of raw strength it is this enigmatic young man, who was born in war-ravaged Europe and later emigrated with his parents to Northern Ontario, Canada.

During a game Tkaczuk is either the irresistible force or the immovable object, depending upon whether he is carrying the puck or stopping an oncoming foe. "Tkaczuk," wrote a Canadian newspaperman, "hard to say, hard to stop." Which is about as accurate as you can put it (the correct pronunciation is "Ka-chook").

Like Stan Mikita, Walter wouldn't have made it to these shores had it not been for the horror of World War II. Mikita came from Communist-controlled Czechoslovakia to Canada, where he was adopted by an uncle and aunt who lived in St. Catherines, Ontario. Tkaczuk's story is a bit more harrowing. His father, Mike, was working in an anthracite mine when German armies moved east on the Soviet Union. The mine was located in the Donets Basin of the Ukraine, directly in the path of the Nazi blitz.

Like many other miners, Mike Tkaczuk was captured by the Wehrmacht and dispatched to Germany, where he was pressed into the Nazi labor force. Unknown to Mike, his eventual bride was in another trainload of Ukrainians heading for the same work camp. After checking Mike's credentials, the German labor officers dispatched him to Emsdetten, a town in the Ruhr Valley near a twelve hundred-foot-deep coal mine. It wasn't the most pleasant place to spend a war, but Mike came out of it intact, got married, and remained in Emsdetten two years after the Nazi surrender.

The unsettled atmosphere of a war-torn country was not the most wholesome in which to raise a child. And after Walter's birth on September 27, 1947, Mike began looking elsewhere for work. Told that miners were needed in Canada, he soon made plans to emigrate and test the lay of the new land across the Atlantic. He headed for South Porcupine, Ontario, found it to his liking, and sent for his wife and infant son. Were it not for that decision, Walter Tkaczuk might be plumbing the depths of a Westphalian mine today.

"I may have grown up in hockey country, but my mother wasn't keen on the sport," Walter once told me. "She had worked hard all her life, just like my father. She didn't think there was any future in hitting a rubber disk around on ice with wooden sticks."

You don't get rich working the northern Ontario mines and Mike Tkaczuk was no exception. Every penny had its use, which explains why Walter's mother was so angry at her son whenever he played hockey. Hockey meant injuries, injuries meant stitches, stitches meant going to the doctor, and doctors cost money—money which the Tkaczuk's could ill afford to pay. "One day," Walter recalled, "I got involved in a really rough game and lost a tooth in the action. I was worried about coming home to my mother after that one. When she saw my tooth was missing she shook her head and said, 'more money.' "

Luckily Walter's progress was way ahead of his injuries and by the time he was thirteen NHL scouts had their eyes on him. Lou Passador of the Rangers was one of the first to detect Tkaczuk's special qualities. Inevitably Walter wound up skating for New York's farm team at Kitchener, Ontario, coached by Steve Brklacich, one of the few people in the world whose name is more difficult to figure out than Tkaczuk's.

"I knew the first time I saw him that we had a real prospect for the big club," said Brklacich. "He was strong as an ox and worked harder than any kid I'd ever seen."

Walter had more incentive than most kids. If he didn't make it as a hockey player, his horizons were limited—limited to the gold mines of northern Ontario. Walter had already tasted the underground life, and wasn't particularly fond of making it a career.

"When I worked in the mines I was just a kid," Walter once told me. "I did the odd jobs. For a while I worked as a track man and a pipe-fitter. I mucked the tunnel and put all the debris in a little cart. Sometimes I held the drill they used to search for veins of gold."

While his hockey future remained uncertain, Tkaczuk did make some progress underground. He graduated to the job of dynamite man's assistant, which entailed lugging bulky air drills and heavy cases of dynamite through the narrow mine tunnel. "We'd look for gold by drilling holes in the side of the tunnel," he explained. "Then we'd put sticks of dynamite in the holes, get the blasting caps and fuses, move back, crouch down, and wait. At my age it all seemed like a lot of fun. All you had to do was know how to count. If you used seven sticks of dynamite, you just listened for seven blasts."

One time I asked Walter if there was anything at all that disturbed him about the experience. He finally admitted that one process bugged the hell out of him —taking the cage-like elevator from the surface of the mine down to the bottom of the pit. He would become claustrophobic as he and forty other miners crammed themselves into the cage.

"Before the cage started moving down," said Walter, "we'd try to get as much air as possible into our lungs. The thing that bugged me was that it took an eternity for that blasted elevator to get to the bottom. Meanwhile, we had to stand there all cramped together. Sometimes we went as deep as 3,300 feet.

"You'd think that once we hit bottom it would be cool, like in a cave or something. But it was nothing like that. It was hot and you would get sweaty, and your feet would hurt from walking on the rocks. In a way it was like being in a science fiction movie—dark and scary with bad smells all around. Sometimes it got so stuffy you couldn't wait to get back up again and take a deep breath of fresh air."

Occasionally the claustrophobia was countered by the fascination of digging for gold. But the search was always more exciting than the find. "Gold wasn't much to look at," he explained. "The color was a dull yellow. It was jagged and crumby-looking; nothing like what you would dream about. And when you touched it, it usually fell apart in your hands."

It was enough to make a young man turn to hockey, where the gold was brighter and, in the long run, more tangible.

The turnabout came at Kitchener, where Tkaczuk fulfilled Brklacich's fondest hopes. He used his unbridled power like a jackhammer, and his zeal for the puck compensated for deficiencies in other areas. When he was eighteen the Rangers invited him to play in a few exhibition games, and the following September he showed up at the big team's training base at Kitchener. That was the first time I met Walter and, to be honest about it, I had trouble getting to know him. He had come to the team surrounded by considerable fanfare, most of it generated by scouts and those who had watched him burn up the Ontario Hockey Association's Junior A League. In the dressing room he was bashful and silent. He answered reporters' questions reluctantly and seemed to want to crawl under the bench rather than face a battery of New York newsmen. His play on the ice seemed equally constrained. Something was missing. Maybe it was the need for a more relaxed atmosphere, maybe it was more training in the minors.

Whatever it was, Rangers manager Emile Francis decided to ship Tkaczuk down to Buffalo for a few games, just to see how he'd react to a minor-league setting. He played five games for the AHL club and immediately began to unwind. His skating was strong and loose and he had a command of the ice that reminded onlookers of the Tkaczuk of Kitchener days. Walter was called up to the NHL.

Interestingly Walter's growth as a hockey player was appreciated more by his teammates and opponents than by the fans. His style lacked the flamboyance of a Brad Park, the speed of a Gene Carr, or the sensationalism of a Derek Sanderson. But behind Tkaczuk's grim, at times colorless façade was one very solid hockey player.

By 1969–70, Tkaczuk's sophomore season, he had come into his own. He averaged just over a point a game and worked as hard defensively as he did on the attack. The line of Tkaczuk, Bill Fairbairn, and Dave Balon neatly complemented the Rod Gilbert-Jean Ratelle-Vic Hadfield unit. Walter's star was very much on the rise.

But somehow, instead of continuing upward, it seemed to dip a trifle the following season. I'm sure the trading of Balon had a lot to do with it. Dave—or "Bozey," as he was known to his teammates—was a workmanlike left wing who had a knack for converting Walter's passes into goals. He scored thirty-six goals in 1970-71 and Walter had forty-nine assists. A year later, with Balon gone, Walter's assist total dropped to forty-two and his point total fell from seventy-five to sixty-six. He did, however, improve in another department, one that may have been just as important. Walter began emerging from the protective shell he had built around himself as a rookie. Newspapermen who had covered him back in September 1968 marveled at how lucid he had become in his answers, how he seemed to welcome interviewers rather than shy away from them, and how he seemed to enjoy the give-and-take of a conversation with teammates and outsiders alike.

For the first time I learned that Walter had a sense of humor, as Brad Park had been telling me all along. One of the best sight gags of the 1972–73 season was his wide-brimmed hat, described by Hugh Delano of the *New York Post* as "an Australian bushwacker's hat or the safari hat worn by Johnny Weissmuller in the old Jungle Jim flicks."

Tkaczuk's hat became a *cause célèbre* by midseason. "They can laugh at the hat all they want," said Walter. "It doesn't bother me, because the hat has brought me luck."

Once Walter wore the hat to the Garden and it attracted a couple of dubious types who told Tkaczuk they really liked his hat. In fact, they seemed to like it enough to want to take it right off his head. "You should have seen Walter beat it out of there," said his pal Park. "He thought they might mug him just to get his hat. Walter really loves that thing."

Walter's wife, Valerie, doesn't share this attachment. One night in February 1973 Valerie saw a grand opportunity to once and for all get rid of the chapeau. She was minding the hat while the Rangers were playing the Atlanta Flames. The moment Peter Stemkowski scored the third goal of his three-goal hat trick, Valerie picked up the hat and sailed it on to the ice. Walter couldn't believe his eyes. Before the cleaning men could pick it up, Walter dashed to his hat and rescued it from the junk heap.

That was about the time Walter was also preventing a less than sensational season from turning into a completely mediocre campaign. In the beginning Walter was joined by speedy Gene Carr on his left wing and determined Billy Fairbairn on his right. Carr, a centerman by trade, seemed to have trouble meshing gears with the other two. Finally coach Francis inserted rookie Steve Vickers on the left wing when Carr was injured and the line did a complete about-face.

"Let's face it," Walter told me, "I wasn't happy about the way things had been going. But by February my game reached its proper level and I was getting a lot more shots on goal, especially from the slot. And our line spent more time in the other end of the rink than in our own."

There had been suggestions that one of Walter's problems was complacency. Like other Rangers, he signed a long-term contract during the summer of 1972 that amounted to nearly ten times the $14,000 he was paid in 1970. But the miner's son insists that money has nothing to do with his performance on the ice.

"When I got the good contract," he said, "I felt a

need to show the club I was worth it. They showed they had confidence in me and that gave me the incentive to do better."

Not that he needed incentive. As far as the other teams are concerned, Walter does more harm, while scoring fewer points, than the more point-producing forwards. His repertoire includes not only taking a regular shift, but Tkaczuk and Bill Fairbairn comprise one of the most efficient penalty-killing combos in the league. "Those are the bulldogs I sic at them," Francis said before giving up coaching.

The Bruins found out the hard way during the 1973 playoffs. A year earlier Boston goalie Ed Johnston had come up with the "book" on Tkaczuk's style. He put it this way:

"Tkaczuk can shoot the puck and he has a fast delivery. He's big and strong and does the sort of thing Phil Esposito does for us. He barges right into the goalmouth. So while you're trying to keep your eye on the puck, there's a hell of a wrestling match going on right on your doorstep."

Walter controlled Esposito in the 1972 finals, but Phil managed to get his passes to wingmen Ken Hodge and Wayne Cashman, who did the destructive scoring. But the 1973 Boston–New York confrontation was another story—all good for Walter and all bad for Phil.

The Esposito–Tkaczuk battle was like a dual between two superb pitchers in the World Series—one with a blazing fastball, the other with a crafty curve. Esposito was the most prolific scorer in contemporary hockey, one who had mastered the keyhole situation,

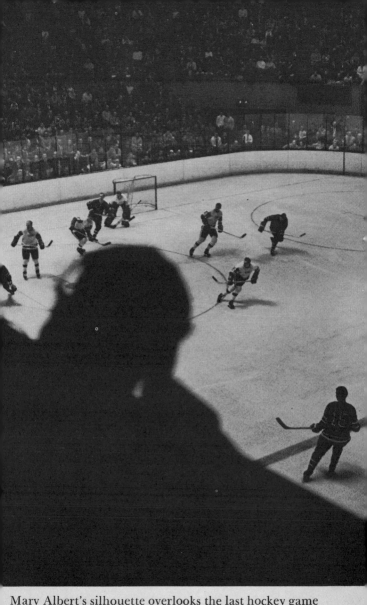

Marv Albert's silhouette overlooks the last hockey game
ever played in the old Madison Square Garden
(Rangers vs. Detroit Red Wings, February 11, 1968).

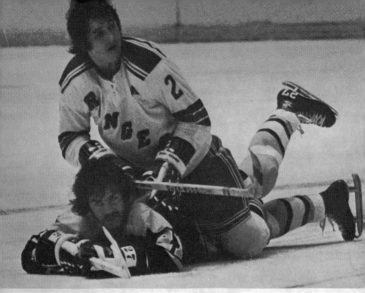

Boston Bruins' Derek Sanderson gets a taste
of the Brad Park treatment. (ROBERT BOREA)

"He scores!" Marv Albert shouts from the
broadcast booth as Billy Fairbairn,
Walt Tkaczuk, and Rod Seiling
go into their victory dance. (BARTON SILVERMAN)

Goalie Ed Giacomin raises puck in triumph
after last year's historic 4-0 shutout of
the Boston Bruins, his first ever in Stanley
Cup playoffs. In background, Marv Albert
joins in the standing ovation. (BARTON SILVERMAN)

"ED-DIE, ED-DIE!" Giacomin responds to the
chants of the crowd and to Bruin Wayne Cashman's
shot as he records one of his 33 saves that night. (UPI)

During his last season behind the bench for the
New York Rangers, Coach Emile Francis finds a few
choice words for the referee. In foreground is
Steve Vickers, Rookie of the Year. (BARTON SILVERMAN)

Ranger center Jean Ratelle leads
the attack down ice while Vic Hadfield
covers the left wing. (ROBERT BOREA)

who with Ken Hodge and Wayne Cashman comprised one of the most feared units in NHL history. Tkaczuk, the defensive specialist, was big like Esposito, but patient enough to allow the Bruin ace to wear himself down before moving in for the kill. For two games Esposito was totally handcuffed while the Rangers swiftly moved to a commanding two-game lead. Moreover, the Bruins were permanently damaged when Esposito was smashed amidships by Rangers defenseman Ron Harris and suffered a severe knee injury. Walter and the Rangers went on to defeat the Bruins in five games, while Esposito was hospitalized for the remainder of the playoffs.

It was now on to Chicago, and Tkaczuk was not to be denied. In the opening game of the semifinals at Chicago Stadium Walter scored two major goals in the third period to salt away the win for New York, 4–1. On top of that Walter limited Chicago center Stan Mikita to only a pair of shots on goal. "This is one of the best-disciplined teams you'll ever see," said Mikita, with a special nod to his adversary, Tkaczuk.

The Black Hawks won the second game, 2–1. Walter scored the Rangers' only goal, and it was truly a gem. Skating alone, he bore down on the Chicago defense of Doug Jarrett and Phil Russell. Using his brute force to his best advantage, Tkaczuk careened past them and lifted a high backhander past goalie Tony Esposito.

From Tkaczuk it was all in a day's work—the kind of play you'd expect from a jet-propelled bulldozer.

10. ED GIACOMIN, THE GOALTENDER'S GOALTENDER

It has been said, and rightly so, that Jacques Plante revolutionized the art of goaltending. Plante was the first goalie to wear a mask and the first to wander behind his net to field the puck so that his defensemen could easily gather it in for a rush up the ice.

But if Plante revolutionized goaltending, Ed Giacomin revolutionized Plante's technique. In short, Giacomin is the first goalie to double as a defenseman. What Plante did was *stop* the puck behind his net, allowing the defensemen to take it from there. But Giacomin has refined the process by passing the puck forward. In effect, Eddie has become the quarterback who sets the play in motion by delivering the first key pass.

Of all Giacomin's enemies, none is more formidable than Derek Sanderson. Yet it was Sanderson who quickly pinpointed Giacomin's value to the New York battle formation. "There's no question," said Sanderson, "that when Giacomin is on the ice the Rangers have three defensemen."

What this means is that the Rangers' other two defensemen on the ice at the time are free to move into attacking position because they know that Giacomin is capable of delivering as precise and crisp a pass up front as any of them. At the moment when the enemy loses the puck and Giacomin retrieves it, the Rangers, in effect, have an extra man on the ice.

Although many observers believe this offensive-goaltending style was recently developed by Giacomin, the fact is he actually started experimenting with the system when he played minor-league goal for Providence during the 1964–65 season.

"There's something inside me that wants to do a little extra," Eddie once explained. "It's part of my temperament."

This experimenting wouldn't have lasted long had Giacomin not played for a sympathetic coach and manager. But when he signed with the Rangers in 1965–66 his coach, Red Sullivan, encouraged him. Later, so did Emile Francis. They realized that Giacomin's roaming was conducive to his style of play.

"Eddie's one of the strongest skaters on the club," said Francis. "Most people think a player becomes a goalie because he can't skate well. Actually strong skating is a prime asset for a goalie."

Since Giacomin's puck-fielding-and-passing movements were, in fact, revolutionary, it is not surprising to discover that Eddie's teammates in those early years had more than a few uneasy moments while adjusting to his free-wheeling style. "He would give me heart failure," said captain Vic Hadfield. "But now I'm used to his brand of goaltending. He can turn things around. The way he moves the puck gives our whole offense a lift."

Of course a goalie's first job is blocking pucks, and in those first seasons Giacomin had his problems. At the start of the 1966–67 season Eddie fell on evil times. The Rangers were losing and he was allowing too many goals per game. After one especially miserable contest, the balcony fans at the old Madison Square Garden could contain their frustration no longer and bombarded Giacomin with garbage.

Livid with anger, manager Francis rallied to his goaltender's side. "The next time they throw garbage at you," snapped Francis, "you just pick it up and throw it right back at them."

This was Giacomin's biggest crisis. He was fronting a relatively weak team and was being pursued for the goaltending job by tall Cesare Maniago. At the time Maniago was given an even-money chance of displacing Giacomin. On November 9, 1966, it appeared that Giacomin had had it with the Rangers. Francis put the popular Maniago in front of the net. If Cesare played well, he had the job.

The Rangers were skating against the Boston Bruins that night. Early in the second period a Bruins shot smacked into Maniago's face mask, sending him reeling to the ice. The disoriented goalie was helped from the rink to a chorus of appreciative cheers. Seconds later his replacement, Giacomin, skated out to a chorus of boos.

Eddie played through the end of the second period, and was still being hooted when the buzzer sounded ending the middle frame. At that point Francis expected Maniago to return. He figured Cesare had had time enough to recover and that Giacomin should be spared any further harassment from the surly crowd. But Maniago claimed that his mouth still bothered him and asked out of the assignment. Unhappy as he was about the crowd, Giacomin valiantly moved back between the pipes and finished the game. But in the process he allowed two goals to elude him. The Rangers 3–1 lead evaporated into a 3–3 tie—and Giacomin left the ice inundated by missiles.

One might assume that Maniago had won his job back by default; but anyone who assumed that didn't know Francis' stubborn nature and his extrasensory perception of a real competitor. "When I played goal," said the little manager, "I wouldn't have let anybody take my place if I could help it. As far as I was concerned, Giacomin was my goalkeeper."

That was the most important decision of Francis' career as Rangers boss. If Giacomin had failed him, the Rangers might have sunk to new depths.

Once Giacomin realized that Francis was completely in his corner he responded with a 110-percent effort. "Emile told me things about goaltending that I had never heard before," said Giacomin.

Eddie also studied the masters—Plante and Terry Sawchuk. By watching Plante he learned the fine points of roaming. "Sawchuk showed me something else," said Giacomin. "He was the first goalie I had ever seen who skated to the bench and exchanged on the fly with a forward when the other team was in a delayed penalty situation."

By the end of November 1966 the crisis was over. Giacomin had played capably and sometimes sensationally. No longer did the diehards throw garbage at him. He finished the season with nine shutouts and a 2.61 goals-against average. Francis was delighted and Maniago was finished.

The manager kept working with his protégé but, significantly, never stopped him from playing his aggressive, "third defenseman" game. After all, it was part of Francis' philosophy as well as Giacomin's.

"I learned my goaltending from Tiny Thompson, the great old Bruins goalie," said Francis. "I was an eighteen-year-old kid in Moose Jaw, Saskatchewan, at the time. Tiny told me a goalie should work at learning to move the puck, that he should be able to pass as well as any defenseman."

But Giacomin had one ambition that had probably never crossed Thompson's or Francis' mind—to score a goal. Eddie's theory was that such a feat would be possible in the final minute of a game with the Rangers leading by a goal and the face-off deep in Rangers territory.

The other team would pull its goalie in favor of a sixth attacker and, somehow, the puck would fall on Giacomin's stick. He then would fire the rubber down the ice into the yawning cage. It was a pleasant enough dream but not one that anyone ever thought would be fulfilled—until one night during the 1969–70 season.

Eddie was in goal that dramatic night in Toronto's Maple Leaf Gardens. The scenario was ideal for the realization of his dream. New York was ahead by a goal. There was a minute to go and Toronto had pulled goalie Bruce Gamble. The puck was dropped at the face-off and it skittered to Giacomin. He didn't fire it directly at the Leaf net but, rather, banked a clearing shot off the sideboard's glass.

For a few seconds it looked like the perfect billiard shot. After bounding off the glass the puck slid tantalizingly toward the Toronto net with not a Leaf in sight to intercept it. There was enough momentum behind the drive to carry it all the way; whether the clearing shot was on target was the only question.

It wasn't. But it was close—so close that the puck nicked a piece of the goalcrease at the right side of the net before glancing off the cage. "I wasn't trying to score," said Giacomin. "My main thought was getting the puck out of trouble. Naturally when the puck got closer and closer to the net, I was hoping it would go in. Wouldn't that have been something?"

With each passing season it became more and more apparent that Francis' faith in Giacomin helped propel the Rangers to the heights. He was not only a goaltender and a third defenseman, but an acknowledged leader to whom the players could turn in a crisis.

"He's one of the best quarterbacks in the game," said Francis, "the kind of leader and holler guy you need for a winner."

By the 1972–73 season Giacomin reached a peak that would have seemed impossible back in the doldrum days of '66. On the night of January 3, 1973, I was fortunate enough to see and broadcast the game in which Eddie broke the Rangers' shutout record.

When Giacomin reached forty shutouts, he had tied the Rangers record held by Davey Kerr, who had tended goal for the New Yorkers from 1934 to 1941. Then on January 3, while seventeen and a half thousand fans watched in amazement, the Los Angeles Kings tossed some of the best shots of the year at Giacomin. On several occasions I felt that I was about to blurt out the words, "The Kings shoot; SCORE!"

In fact, with 9:39 remaining in the second period, the words just about flowed out of my mouth. The Rangers were ahead, 1–0, and Los Angeles had a power play in motion. The puck came to the Kings' Bob Berry at the slot. He let go a blazer that seemed earmarked for the open corner. But Giacomin's skate got there first and he brushed it aside.

The save forced him to his right, leaving a huge opening to his left. Unfortunately for Eddie the puck rebounded to Juha Widing, who just happened to be ten feet in front of the net with the puck on his stick. There were no Rangers defensemen in sight.

Widing's sure goal was about a foot off the ice as it headed toward the gaping net. Everyone in the building thought it was goal—everyone, that is, but Giacomin. "It sure looked like an open net and an easy goal from where I was standing," said Francis.

As the puck orbited in front of the net, Giacomin flung his body in the opposite direction from where his original save had carried him. His left catching glove and the rubber got to the red goal line at the same time. Eddie had blocked the puck.

I was flabbergasted by the save, but no more so than the Kings. They couldn't believe Giacomin's magic and automatically assumed that the puck *had* passed him. But referee Bryan Lewis brushed aside their futile protests. After the game Eddie pieced together the second-by-second events.

"Berry's shot threw me off balance as I made the save. At that point I saw Widing with the puck and thought he'd just slide it in. I reached back with my hand when he started to shoot. The puck hit me in the arm and dropped to the ice. But it never went in."

The big save on Widing left the seventeen and a half thousand fans thoroughly exhausted. "I heard the hush of the crowd," said Eddie. "I guess they thought the puck was in the net. When I raised my head and saw it there, two or three inches away from the goal line, I knew the fans didn't realize that it hadn't gone in."

If the Kings couldn't score on that kind of chance, they wouldn't score on any other kind of shot that night. And when it was over Giacomin was toasted by the roars of the appreciative crowd. Later, when I interviewed him, he said that his record-breaking performance was one of the most satisfying moments in his goaltending career.

"For me it's a very, very great honor to be known as the best goaltender in Rangers history," he said.

The Widing shot wasn't Giacomin's only exceptional moment. But it was easily the most exceptional save on the most exceptional of nights. At other times he received more help from his teammates, such as the night in March when Rod Seiling saved a goal and prevented a Rangers loss.

The play started when Rick MacLeish of the Philadelphia Flyers burst through the Rangers defense, lured Giacomin out of position, and slid the puck toward the open cage. "It went behind me," said Giacomin, "and I thought to myself, 'Oh God!'" Once again it appeared that nothing could prevent the puck from entering the cage. Nothing but Seiling. He dashed across the goal mouth, dropped to his right knee, and kicked the puck to the left side. "When I saw him shoot," Seiling explained to me later, "I knew Eddie was in trouble and that I had to back him up. It's hard to say how I knew, but it just came to me—like that!"

I am often asked what makes Giacomin such an exceptional goaltender. Part of it is his skating and puck control, part of it his superb reflexes. Emile Francis calls it a "natural instinct." The ex-NHL goalie explained, "Eddie always knows where the puck is or where it's going."

Others say it's his combative nature. Giacomin will fight for the area around his crease. He once challenged Derek Sanderson, and another time put a hammerlock around Jacques Plante during a melee with the Maple Leafs. During the 1972–73 season I was broadcasting the game when Eddie and his old teammate Cesare Maniago grappled with each other like a pair of elephants.

The fight started when Bill Goldsworthy of the Minnesota North Stars collided with Eddie behind the Rangers net. Goldsworthy didn't mean any harm and skated away from the scene thinking the trouble was over. "The next thing I knew," said Goldsworthy,

"Giacomin was skating after me waving that big stick of his."

Eddie was angry because Goldsworthy had hit him on the wrist with his stick. "I wanted to get him back," said Giacomin, "and that's why I went after him."

Eddie caught up to Goldsworthy and then all hell broke loose. Dale Rolfe rushed in to get Goldsworthy, and then Dennis Hextall jumped Rolfe. Giacomin went after Hextall, and Doug Mohns, who was heading for Giacomin, was grabbed by Vic Hadfield. Finally Maniago decided to get into the act and he skated from his goal crease, eventually landing on top of Giacomin in what was one of the wildest two-goalie confrontations I've ever seen.

"The minute I saw Giacomin get into the fight," said Maniago, "I knew that I had to get into it. I didn't mean to start any more trouble; all I wanted to do was cool down Eddie. As soon as I wrestled him to the ice, I told him to take it easy or he'd get fined. I didn't mean any harm. After all, we're old friends."

Maniago isn't the only guy who likes Eddie. Giacomin has become old friends with the fans who jam the Garden for every home game. By playoff time 1973 they had taken him to their hearts. Whenever he has a hot night, which is often, the chants of ED-DIE, ED-DIE begin.

Those cascading cheers are much more pleasant to the graying goaltender than the cascading garbage that once nearly ended his career with the Rangers. "He is," said columnist Gene Ward of the *Daily*

News, "the policeman who makes the whole end of the rink his precinct."

He is the goaltender's goaltender. No higher praise can be delivered for Eddie Giacomin.

11. STEVE VICKERS, THE NEW BREED

The difference between the Rangers and the big, bad Boston Bruins from the 1966–67 season when Bobby Orr entered the NHL was the difference between the thoughtful student and the schoolyard bully.

With tough characters such as Ted Green, Wayne Cashman, John McKenzie, Derek Sanderson, Don Awrey, Don Marcotte, and Ken Hodge, the Bruins intimidated most of the smaller teams in the league. The Rangers weren't exactly tiny, but they weren't as brutal nor as aggressive as the Boston skaters.

I remember smallish Rangers such as Dave Balon getting creamed by the likes of Green with little hope of retaliation. Who can forget the mammoth brawl between the Bruins and Rangers in the 1970 Stanley Cup playoff when Sanderson sucker-punched Billy Fairbairn? Or the time in the 1972 Cup final when Derek doubled over Rod Gilbert with an illegal knee in the stomach?

Mind you, the Rangers got in their licks. They weren't patsies for the Bruins or any other big team. But when it came right down to elbows and kneecaps,

New York just didn't have the likes of a Hodge or Cashman.

Then along came Steve Vickers and everything changed. It was on a Saturday night, February 3, 1973, in the Boston Garden. Before then Don Marcotte of the Bruins had spent a good deal of his NHL career knocking over Rangers. This time Vickers laid him out on the ice in such convincing fashion only those few who knew Steve's tough fibre were not surprised. The Rangers general manager Emile Francis was one of those few. "Vickers is tough," Francis had told me. "It takes a lot to get him riled up, but when he does, look out!"

Rangers scout Steve Brklacich remembered Vickers as a junior left wing. He was the strong, silent type, with the accent on the "strong." "No guy in his right mind messed with him when he played junior hockey," said Brklacich. "Steve was a different kind of fighter; he didn't start fights, he just finished them. He put a lot of guys on their backsides with that right hand of his."

The mashing of Marcotte was only the first of several battles between Vickers and members of the opposition. But as a rookie in the 1972–73 season he received his share of blows. There was a hard-fought draw in the playoffs with Ken Hodge that impressed the Bruins only because Hodge almost never loses a fight.

Curiously Vickers' fighting ability was only a minor factor in Steve's rise to fame with the Rangers. His scoring and his uncanny knack for being in the right place at the right time were also invaluable assets. In the Fall of 1972 Dave Balon had been traded away, and Francis was on the prowl for a left wing to work with Walt Tkaczuk and Bill Fairbairn. At the time Gene Carr was holding down the left wing spot.

"Carr hadn't been scoring," Francis told me, "so I thought about putting Steve on the line. I remembered that Vickers had been a left-handed right winger in junior hockey. When we got him we sent him to our farm team in Omaha with instructions to play him at left wing. He got thirty-six goals down there, so I knew he could put the puck in the net."

There were seventeen thousand five hundred witnesses to substantiate Francis' claim on Saturday afternoon, November 11, 1972, when Vickers took his place on left wing with Tkaczuk and Fairbairn against the California Golden Seals. The husky Vickers, who has been likened to the character Alex in the film *A Clockwork Orange,* scored one goal and worked well with Tkaczuk and Fairbairn. The Rangers won, 7–2.

"Each could have had two or three more goals," said Francis. "It was marvelous to watch them move that puck around, in and out of the corners."

Suddenly Vickers was in the headlines. "The year-long search to find a replacement for Balon may have ended," said Mark Ruskie in the Bergen (New Jersey) *Record.* "Vickers provides something Balon never contributed—muscle."

I myself tended to be more conservative about Steve. I wanted to be shown that his effort against the Seals was no flash in the pan. The next night, when the Rangers took on Los Angeles, I made a point of watching Vickers more closely.

What I saw in those sixty minutes of action left me doing double-takes. The six-foot, 185-pounder from Toronto, Ontario, pumped a three-goal hat trick past Kings goalie Gary Edwards as the Rangers won, 5–1. It was becoming clear that Vickers was not only a fair substitute for Balon, he might just go Dave one better.

"All Walter and Billy ever needed was someone to put the puck in the net," said Brad Park, "and now they've got him. Steve is really something. He goes up and down his wing and is a tough man to move out of there in front. He reminds me of our old captain, Bob Nevin. He doesn't say much, just shrugs his shoulders."

I wasn't about to shrug off Vickers' accomplishment, but after all, these were only a couple of games. I still believed that I had to see more of him. If he scored a goal in the following game at home on November 15 against the Philadelphia Flyers, I'd feel a lot more convinced.

This time I was totally flabbergasted. The twenty-one-year-old rookie had done the impossible. He scored another hat trick to give the Rangers a 7–3 triumph over the Flyers. After his third goal a dozen hats were tossed out on the ice to toast Steve's sensational performance. Vickers appeared to be the calmest person in the building after it was over. I spoke to him later in the dressing room and smiled when I congratulated him. "Marv," he said, "I just hope they don't expect three goals from me in *every* game."

The Rangers had liked Dave Balon, whom they

had nicknamed "Bozey." But Steve was making them forget the sixty-nine goals Dave had scored in two seasons on the Tkaczuk–Fairbairn line. "Steve and Bozey are a lot alike," said Tkaczuk. "They both know how to position themselves, but Steve's a little stronger. You can't push him away. He's strong on his skates and you really have to work to move him."

Fairbairn, one of the quietest athletes in any sport, wouldn't shut up about his new left wing. When Fairbairn says more than a dozen words, you *know* it's important stuff. "Steve always seems to be in front of the net," said Fairbairn. "Walter and I don't even have to look for him when we want to make a pass because we're sure he'll be there."

Needless to say, Vickers was the very soul of modesty about his second straight hat trick. "Let's be fair about it," said Vickers. "Billy and Walter are doing all the work getting the puck to me. It isn't all that hard once you have something to score with."

An injury sidelined Steve for sixteen games in midseason, and I wondered, soon after his return late in December, whether the rookie might skate a bit more timidly through the second half of the schedule. But Steve reacted as if nothing had happened. On February 3, the night that he flattened Marcotte, Vickers scored his twentieth goal of the season, flipping home Tkaczuk's rebound.

That was the signal for Vickers' fans to start talking about rookie-of-the-year honors. Interestingly not all of those fans were New Yorkers. "Vickers has been a dangerous weapon for most of the six weeks that he's been healthy," said Bob Dunn of the *Montreal Star* early in February. "Vickers has the credentials," wrote Hugh Delano in the *New York Post,* "twenty three goals and forty points in forty-five games, the best shooting percentage in the NHL, and a fondness for general warfare in the corners and in front of the net."

Despite the chorus of pro-Vickers chants, Steve seemed to lay low and did as little talking as possible, emulating his linemate Fairbairn. "When Steve and Billy are in the same room," Francis kidded one day, "you have to keep turning around to make sure they're still there."

Meanwhile the opposition goalies kept turning around to fetch the puck from the net as Steve kept firing away. He finished the season with an amazing thirty goals—twenty more than the original target he had set for himself—and had become a celebrity on a team already filled with stars.

"I knew there were stars all around me on this team," Steve told me one night on my *Sportsline* show, "but I tried not to think about that too much. If I did, it would hurt my chances. I told myself that I was as good as they were and that I could make it in the NHL."

The regular season is one thing, but the playoffs are something special. Once again it was the Rangers vs. the Bruins, only this time it was a best-of-seven series in the first round of the Cup competition. Now I thought I'd really know how far Vickers had progressed.

He was held scoreless in the first game, at Boston,

but the Rangers won it, 6–2, for what was regarded as a major upset. It was in the second game that Steve came into his own. With the Bruins leading, 1–0, in the first period, he took passes from Brad Park and Billy Fairbairn and beat goalie Jacques Plante to tie the game for New York. In the second period Ted Irvine and Pete Stemkowski put the Rangers ahead to stay.

It was Vickers who knocked Bruins ace Phil Esposito off-balance, setting the Boston center up for the crunching bodycheck delivered by Ron Harris which sidelined Esposito for the rest of the series. In a sense Vickers' block set the stage for the Rangers' dominance of the series and upset Steve's own forecast that the playoff would go six or seven games. It was this big, tough rookie who also added the final nails to the Bruins' coffin. Only thirty-eight seconds had elapsed in the first period of the fifth and final game when Vickers stunned the crowd of 15,003 with a shot past goalie Ross Brooks to give the Rangers the lead. But the Bruins rebounded for a pair of goals to go ahead, 2–1. For a few moments it appeared that the Stanley Cup champions might pull away. But Vickers scored his second goal of the period at 14:34. Later in the period Bruce MacGregor gave New York the lead again.

With a 5–2 lead in the third period, the Rangers faced one more challenge when Don Marcotte scored for the Bruins, reducing the Rangers' margin to 5–3. Boston Garden was alive again and the Bruins pressed for another score. That's when Mister "Hat Trick"

Vickers did it again. At 17:51 Steve slapped in his third goal of the game to cap a 6–3 Rangers' victory and 4–1 triumph in the series.

Like most fans, I had wondered just what kind of young dynamo this Vickers could be. He had been described as poised and mature beyond his years. Having Steve on my program helped me understand more about the young left wing, and some conversations we had following that enlightened me even more.

Steve grew up in Toronto, the oldest of six children —five boys and a girl. "The others," he said, "are all intellectuals. They're not dummies like me."

His father, a fireman, had never played organized hockey, and Steve didn't get involved seriously in the game until he was nine. "I started thinking seriously about playing pro hockey when I was seventeen," he told me. "I thought that if I was going to play this stupid game, why not get paid for it?"

He played for the Toronto Marlboros in the Ontario Hockey Association Junior A League, and was the Rangers' number one selection in the 1971 amateur draft. Francis made him a pro in 1971–72. At Omaha of the Central Pro League he scored thirty-six goals and twenty-three assists for fifty-nine points in seventy games. He was not given much of a chance to make the big team when he reported to training camp in September 1968, and admitted as much.

"When I arrived in camp," Vickers recalled, "I looked around and figured these were three guys who had a shot at the team before I did—Gene Carr, Tommy Williams, and Curt Bennett. With that in mind, I knew I had to work harder than usual. I had to have a positive attitude if I was going to make the team.

"At first I didn't think I had a chance, but within three days I changed my mind. Once they put me in a scrimmage against the NHL types I realized I could play at their level. I thought I had a job with the big boys, but [Emile] Francis didn't say anything to me until the last day of training camp. When he finally did say something, it was short and sweet: 'You'll be staying here.' "

Even when Steve was called up in 1972, he wasn't getting the kind of ice time he had wanted. Carr was the regular left wing on the Fairbairn–Tkaczuk line.

"I had wanted to be drafted by an expansion team," he admitted, "because I knew that I'd have a better chance of becoming a regular. When I didn't get to play early in my rookie year I began having doubts about my future with the Rangers. The change came when I got on the line with Walter and Billy and got those two hat tricks. Not because I set a record with back-to-back hat tricks, but because they came at a time when I needed them. It showed me once and for all that I could play in this league. I had been wondering for five years whether I was good enough for the NHL. Those hat tricks gave me my answer."

The other answer came in June 1973, when Steve *was* named the NHL's Rookie-of-the-Year!

12. JEAN RATELLE, ARTISTRY ON ICE

It is a violent game, yet he is as mild as an archbishop. It is a game in which blood flows freely, yet he dances through the opposition like a phantom, immune to the blood-letting. He is virtually a saint among stickhandlers, an uncanny artist. He is Jean Ratelle, the complete center who, it often appears, must have written the book about playing his position.

If Ratelle has any drawbacks it is an innate modesty that has kept him from receiving the brand of publicity that less gifted, more voluble centers, such as Derek Sanderson, have received. A French-Canadian, Ratelle hardly spoke a word of English until he moved from his native Montreal to Kitchener, where he played his junior hockey.

His mastery of English came slowly but surely. Today he speaks his "new" language fluently, occasionally salting it with a French epithet or two. His mastery of hockey also came slowly. He had his first full tryout with the Rangers in the 1961–62 season— an abject failure. He scored only four goals and admittedly felt out of place in the NHL.

"Management in New York put a lot of pressure on me," Jean once told me. "They wanted me to play a more aggressive brand of hockey. But that just wasn't the way I played the game. So pretty soon I found myself down in the minors again."

The New York management realized that Jean had the basic skills for being an ace. He had long, easy skating strides and his wrist shot was accurate and inevitably ended up in the corner of the net. And his stickhandling was a dream-come-true for a coach. The trick was to put it all together.

"A season after that first big trial," Jean went on, "they brought me back to New York. This time I felt a lot more comfortable—and it showed in my scoring. I scored eleven goals in forty-eight games in an era when twenty goals was a big accomplishment. But the club wasn't playing all that well, so they sent me back down to the minors—to Baltimore."

That was a time when Jean Beliveau of the Montreal Canadiens was the premier center in all hockey. A publicist in New York who needed some material to boost the Rangers at the time went out on a limb and called Ratelle "the Rangers' answer to Beliveau." It was a very presumptuous statement to make and weighed heavily on Ratelle for some time after that. Especially since he didn't believe he was in Beliveau's class.

"It was impossible for me to ignore the comparisons being made between myself and Beliveau," Ratelle told me. "In a sense I was flattered. But I was realistic about it and I knew that part of the reason was for publicity. I never patterned my style after Beliveau's. So as far as I was concerned, any comparisons were just to give the publicists something to do."

Ironically, exactly ten years to the month after the first comparisons had been made, it was Beliveau himself who praised Ratelle by calling him one of the most accomplished forwards in modern hockey. Beliveau also acknowledged that there was good reason to compare Ratelle's style with his own.

"Sure," said Beliveau, "our styles are similar. We both play very cleanly, we're pretty quiet fellows, and we both have a long skating stride and a long reach."

When Beliveau played for Montreal he was the captain, the acknowledged leader of the famed team known as the "Flying Frenchmen." Ratelle has never captained the Rangers, but in Beliveau's eyes the long, lean Ranger is a leader in his own subtle way.

"The way I see it," said Beliveau, "Jean Ratelle is the quiet leader of the Rangers. It's a mistake to think that a player has to be noisy in order to command respect and lead a hockey club. Jean inspires by his behavior—on and off the ice. He's a fine family man and an inspiration to the other players, especially the younger ones. He reminds me of myself in the sense that neither of us were flashy or noisy or were quoted saying anything controversial, and because of that it took longer to get recognized."

By the 1972–73 season Ratelle had unquestionably been recognized up and down the NHL. On January 29, 1973, he became the fourth player in Ranger history to score 250 goals—the others being Andy Bathgate, Camille Henry, and Rod Gilbert—in a 5–2 win over Toronto.

It seemed that whenever Ratelle lit the red light, it came as a result of a picture play. One time against Toronto Jean was the hero, and Lynn Hudson of the New York *Daily News* put it this way: "Ratelle's goal was the sort of lovely maneuver for which Ratelle has become noted. He skated in alone on goalie Ron Low, forced him to come forward, faked him to the side, and slipped it in the chords."

Every so often the goal would be something less than a classic—as on the night of November 21, 1972, at the Omni in Atlanta. The Rangers won the game, 3–1, and Ratelle's score was the one that gave the Rangers breathing room when they were being threatened with less than three minutes to play.

Jean was standing in front of Atlanta goalie Phil Myre when a shot bounced off his leg and caromed past the Flames netminder. "I was lucky," said Ratelle, "I happened to be in the right place at the right time. The puck just as well could have bounced into the corner of the rink."

By March 23, 1973, Ratelle was the only Ranger within reach of the forty-goal plateau. He had scored forty-six goals the previous season, but it was very unlikely that he, or any NHL player for that matter, could put two forty-goal seasons back to back. Yet on the night of March 23 Ratelle was up against the Flames in Atlanta. Once again the Rangers, despite their 2–1 lead, were being hounded by the Flames, and once again Ratelle got the big goal to ease the pressure—his fortieth. It seemed that Beliveau was as proud of Ratelle's accomplishment as the Rangers center was himself.

"Jean's strong point is his consistency," said Beliveau. "Consistency is what makes a great hockey player, and that's why the Rangers can't afford to be without him. He's so consistent the way he headmans the puck; he's so unselfish, always feeding passes to his two wings."

With Beliveau retired, Ratelle finds himself compared to other classy NHL centers, including the superb Phil Esposito of Boston. I'll always remember their confrontation on the night of January 9, 1972.

It was the thirty-ninth game of the season for the Rangers, the midway mark of the campaign. Jean and Phil were neck and neck in a race for the scoring championship. That was the night Ratelle put on a clutch spurt and took over sole possession of the scoring race by racking up five big points.

Fans have often asked me just what it is about Ratelle's style that has marked him so many cuts above the average center. The answer is not a simple one. It isn't merely his skating ability, his heads-up style of play, or his excellent wrist shot—but a combination of these skills. And the reason for this, in my estimation, is that Jean has had the benefit of a long apprenticeship in the minor leagues. Jean Ratelle was no overnight sensation. He played for Three Rivers (Quebec) in the old Eastern Pro League, in Kitchener, and then spent three seasons with Baltimore in the American League. That's a lot of time to spend down on the farm, but in retrospect Ratelle is far from bitter.

"There's no question in my mind," Jean told me, "that all that time I spent in the minors was a great benefit to me in the long run, although I might not have thought so at the time. A lot of kids coming out of junior hockey make the mistake of thinking they should go straight to the NHL. They're not giving themselves the freedom of practicing new techniques, which you can do better in the minors.

"Nowadays, with so many new teams, it's much easier for a kid to make the jump, but I don't think it's such a smart move. I'm convinced that only a select few are really equipped—mentally and physically —to handle the pace and the pressure of the NHL. I can't point out one or two things that happened to me in the minors that made a difference. It was more of a collective thing."

Jean is the first to admit that he got help elsewhere. Rod Gilbert, his chum from childhood days at Academie Roussin in Montreal, was the first to point out Jean's ability to the people in Guelph, Ontario, where Rod was playing junior hockey. It was Gilbert (and Vic Hadfield) who, in part, was responsible for Ratelle's winning the West Side Association's Players' Player award for four consecutive years, from 1968 through 1971. "I don't care how many points Ratty has," teammate Ted Irvine once said, "it won't change him. That's the beautiful thing about the guy. He's something extra. He's all class. He never thinks about himself, no matter how great he really is."

Larry Merchant of the New York *Post* put it this way in his daily sports column: "Ratelle is a pure skater in the tradition of French-Canadians, as best exemplified by the Montreal Canadiens. He is the kind of hockey player all the ruffians would be if they had the ability. He is fast, clever, intelligent, and most of all, he is in full control of himself and the puck as the hurly-burly whooshes around him in apparent disorder."

I would paraphrase Merchant this way: when you're watching Jean Ratelle in action, you are seeing sheer artistry on ice.

13. THE OFF-SIDE OF THE RANGERS

The difference between the Rangers you see on the ice and their behavior off the ice is similar to the difference between one's personality in school and at home, or the difference between the way a person behaves behind the desk at his office and how he reacts at the dinner table.

Hockey players are people, and like people anywhere, there are many sides to their personalities. The fans usually have only one side available to them—the one visible at the game. Newspapermen and broadcasters such as myself are able to see some of their other faces—in the dressing room, on the airplanes and occasionally at home.

For example, defenseman Rod Seiling is a good neighbor of mine. Every so often Rod will visit my house in Long Island and play a game of one-on-one basketball with me in my backyard. The hard-pressing Rod Seiling of my basketball court is far different from the cool Rod Seiling of the hockey rink. But, of most significance to me, Rod still hasn't mastered the jump-shot. Pete Stemkowski, on the other hand, appears to be a very serious center, consumed with face-offs and bodychecks. Off ice he is the team clown. The Stemmer, as he's known to the players, is the Henny Youngman of hockey, a master of the one-liner and not a bad mimic either. He can toss a John Wayne or a Kirk Douglas at you as easy as he throws a pass, and he's never been known to stifle a needle, especially when it's directed at his teammates. I recall him walking to the team bus one night, affecting a severe limp and a Knute Rockne monologue, "I'm playin' hurt tonight, guys: that's the difference between superstars and your ordinary run-of-the-mill star."

Seiling is intense and serious by nature. Perhaps it is a function of his position on the team. Unlike the flashier players such as Brad Park and Rod Gilbert, Seiling has spent most of his career in the background, efficiently doing his work with a minimum of flair and publicity.

"Defensemen like Seiling are never appreciated until they are hurt," said Hall of Famer Tom Johnson, who starred for years on the Montreal Canadiens defense. "They're overlooked, taken for granted because they're steady but not spectacular like a Bobby Orr. But when they're not around, you suddenly realize how valuable they really are." In fact, players around the league will tell you Rod Seiling is one of the most valuable players on the Rangers.

When Seiling was injured late in the 1972–73 season he was replaced by a player of a similar disposition, Ron Harris. Workmanlike, same as Seiling, Harris nevertheless stunned the NHL by grabbing headline after headline during the playoff series with Boston. It was one of those rare cases of a second-stringer clicking on all cylinders. Does anyone remember how Dusty Rhodes did it as a pinch-hitter for the New York Giants years and years ago? Well that's how it was for Harris.

How does one account for Harris' sudden emergence from obscurity to become the subject of eight-column headlines? Doug Gilbert of the Montreal *Gazette* had an interesting observation:

"Harris shows all the signs of being one of those athletes who performs like a journeyman most of the time and then rises to tremendous heights with the pressure at the highest. He's just the reverse of the season-long superstar who gets a lump in the playoffs and contributes nothing."

During the 1973 New York–Boston series, Harris attracted Bruins to his husky body like flies to molasses. One by one the Bruins went down in a heap, including the prize catch, Phil Esposito, who was hospitalized after their collision. I asked Ron how he accounted for his play in the Boston series.

"Remember," Ron told me, "I had been in only two playoff series in ten years, so I was really turned on more than some guys who had been in several Cup rounds. Maybe that's why the Bruins series was the best I ever had and the most satisfying. After all, I've been a benchwarmer for most of my career; either a fifth defenseman or a fourth-line winger. Considering that, you can understand how hard I tried when Emile Francis made me a regular."

The other Ron Harris type was Glen Sather, nicknamed "Slats," who was a utility forward all season, waiting for an emergency to win a regular spot in the lineup. The two players are opposite in personality. Harris is just as quiet in the dressing room or on the plane as he is on the ice. Sather is talkative, funny, and interested in things other than hockey. As Glen once put it, "I could never just play and think hockey all the time. I'd be pretty dull if I did. An athlete needs outside interests just like any other working guy."

One of Sather's avocations is child psychology. "I want to understand children better," he explained. "Kids are where it's at today. Besides, I run a hockey school in Alberta during the off-season, and it helps me understand the kids I work with."

Glen is one of the growing number of big-leaguers who are or have attended college. He worked out an interesting deal with the Detroit Red Wings, his original owners, when he was only twenty years old. Sather signed with the Detroiters only after they agreed to finance his college education. Once, when he was a guest on my "Sportsline" show, I asked him about the deal.

"They had to pay my way to summer school until I got a degree," Glen told me. "And all that was required from me was to be playing in the NHL. I was entitled to room and board, tuition, plus fifty dollars a week spending money. It was for security. When I made the deal in 1964 kids couldn't get bonuses to play hockey, so I figured that this was the next best way to assure my education."

Glen still hasn't completed all his courses, but he has learned enough about psychology to disrupt the opposition more often than most players. "You'd be surprised the things you can put to work in the NHL once you begin to develop an understanding of what makes people tick and why they do the things they do," he said. "If you can get an opponent upset, you've gone a long way toward beating him. If he loses his temper, he won't be concentrating on his real job, which is playing hockey. So I study the opposition and figure out ways to rile them and throw them off-balance."

Some of his ploys are subtle. Sports editor Jim Proudfoot of the *Toronto Star* detected a few of what he called Sather's gimmicks. "Glen," said Proudfoot, "has an evil little smirk which can be infuriating. He specializes in those irritating little fouls which escape the referee's attention and he has an incessant line of patter which can drive an adversary wild with rage."

Once Glen got his comeuppance during an appearance on my "Sportsline" show. He received a call from a man who obviously had a bone to pick. "I sent my boy to your hockey school," the caller snapped. "The kid didn't learn to skate and didn't learn a thing about hockey. I want my money back!"

Momentarily stunned, Glen pulled himself together when he realized the man behind the disguised voice was none other than captain Vic Hadfield!

In contrast to the animated Sather is Bill Fairbairn, who says less in one season than Sather says in one sitting. Yet nobody in the NHL plays harder on the ice than "Billy the Bulldog." He has become the perfect example of an honest hockey player—a wing who skates as hard defensively as he does offensively and who, along with linemate Walt Tkaczuk, has mastered the art of penalty-killing. But Fairbairn is not a showboat, and for that reason the newsmen file him in the drawer marked "bad copy."

Compare him with Gene Carr, who scored forty-four fewer points than Fairbairn during the 1972–73 season. Yet Carr got forty-four per cent more coverage. The answer, as you may have guessed, has to do with "color." Gene Carr, whatever you may think of him as a player, oozes with excitement. He knows it and the fans know it.

"It's kind of scary," said Gene, "but everyone seems to notice everything I do out there on the ice."

His long blond hair helps. His lightning speed helps. His looks help. He is, as we say in this business, dripping with sex appeal. I made that discovery when he appeared on "Sportsline." We received an unusually high number of calls from young girls.

Needless to say, Carr's superstud image has turned off some of the more conservative fans and has given the opposition something to needle him about. The easy way out would have been to cut his hair and become more like the typical hockey player. But Gene would never do that. He is, like Derek Sanderson, his own man. "It wouldn't matter whether I scored seventy goals or seven goals," said Gene, "I'm not going to change my personality. No matter who you are or what you do, you have to be your own man and do your own thing. And that, take it or leave it, is what I'm doing."

Another who won't change his personality is defenseman Jim Neilson, a Ranger who year in and year out is criticized for not being aggressive enough for his size (6-2, 200 pounds). "After all these years," said Jimmy, "I'm tired of hearing that I don't use my weight enough. What people don't realize is that my temperament is such that I don't go flying off the handle very often."

Some players do change—if not their personality, at least their style of play. Rod Gilbert has become more of a hitter at right wing while left wing, Vic Hadfield, has smoothed out a lot of the rough edges that had hampered his play in earlier seasons. "I really wasn't a very good skater when I made it to the NHL," said Vic, "and I didn't score that much. I had to make this up by aggressiveness. In those days whenever we played Montreal our line was pitted against Henri Richard's line. Our job wasn't to score, just to stop their line. We figured it was Henri who made that line go, and my job was to stop him. I really didn't know how. The only thing I knew how to do was take a run at him. So that's what I did. That made up for a lot of things. I've changed quite a bit since then. The big thing is that I've learned to control myself. Now I think before I take a run at somebody. I haven't softened up; it's just that I pick my shots when I know it won't hurt the team."

Speaking of shots, nobody in the Ranger family is more familiar with shots in the mouth, shots in the jaw, and shots in the head than trainer Frank Paice, who now is in his twenty-sixth year of treating the Rangers' wounds. Paice joined the Blueshirts' staff in March 1948 after serving two years as trainer for the Rovers.

He has handled everything from broken collarbones

to split fingers, and has told me that hockey players are the toughest of all professional athletes. According to Paice, it all has to do with a youngster's upbringing. As soon as a boy is old enough to walk in Canada, he's put on skates, and by age three he's playing a variation of hockey.

"By the time he's five years old," Paice continued, "he's been belted to the ice by hard bodychecks, banged against the boards, and bruised and cut by pucks, sticks, and skates. And, of course, there's always those flying elbows and well-aimed fists.

"In the United States the kids imitate pro baseball and football players. In Canada, where hockey is the national sport, the kids play the game the way their NHL heroes do. If they see a player get cut and keep on playing, they do the same. If a player gets slashed and retaliates by punching an opponent, they'll do the same.

"The kids in Canada, who are the NHL stars of the future, learn to live with pain. They grow up ignoring minor injuries and tolerating the more painful ones. Just like it is with us in the majors, hockey is their way of life, not just a game."

Over the years Paice is usually the one who does the stitching. But during the 1972–73 season the situation was reversed. It happened during a Rangers–Sabres game while Paice was standing in his accustomed spot near the sideboards.

"All of a sudden," Paice recalled, "Peter Stemkowski came along, chasing a Buffalo player. He passed right by the bench, and in the heat of the action his stick came over the boards and caught me above the eye. It took four stitches to close the gash, but I came right back to the bench."

Frank doesn't buy the theory that today's high-priced players are softer than the ones who skated for New York twenty to twenty-five years ago. "We've got some rugged players on this club," he said. "During the 1972–73 season we had guys playing who shouldn't have even been in the Garden as spectators."

A man who has been around the Rangers as long as Paice inevitably waxes nostalgic about some of the heroes of yesteryear—the ones who required the most embroidery from his talented needle. He remembers two above all as heroic, and another pair as less than stout fellows.

"Among the old-timers," said Paice, "goalie Chuck Rayner and defenseman Lou Fontinato were two of the gutsiest. Rayner had 207 stitches in his face and head alone and never complained. Of course in those days goalies didn't wear protective face masks. Fontinato would play as long as he could stand up. And no matter how much he hurt he never complained.

"Some years later Max Bentley joined the Rangers. He was a fantastic stickhandler and skater, but he always thought he was sick. The more Max complained, the better he played. After Max left, Jacques Plante came along, and he always seemed to be hurt in some way or another, yet he rarely missed a game. Like Max, Jacques played his best hockey when he was complaining."

14. THE GREAT ALL-TIME RANGERS

Who were the greatest Rangers? I have had this question tossed at me a hundred times during my broadcasting career, and no book about the Rangers would be complete without an All-Time Rangers team of some sort. Yet the Rangers' history spans the better part of five decades, and it would be unfair and impractical to pick an All-Star team without taking into account the evolution of hockey over the years.

The fans of today would hardly recognize the game of hockey as it was played in the late twenties, and the styles and the skills of the players were a reflection of the era in which they played. Moreover, it would be just as unfair to compare the Stanley Cup-winning Rangers of 1928 and 1940 with players during the lean years. An All-Star must be picked relative to his value to the team and relative to the era in which he played.

The only fair way to solve this problem and to give credit where credit is due is to pick *more* than one All-Ranger team. Which is exactly what I've done. In fact I have picked four teams, each team representing the cream of the crop, in my opinion, during four distinct eras in Ranger history. Most of the players you have encountered in previous chapters, and if you have been reading closely you can guess most of my picks from what I have already said about them.

The first team will be called The Originals and will be chosen from the time of the club's formation by Conn Smythe and then Lester Patrick through the mid-thirties.

My second category will be titled The Prewar (World War II) Aces and will be made up of players who were on the team from 1936 through 1942, the year when most of the best Rangers enlisted in the armed forces.

The third grouping, The Postwar Era, takes in players active from 1946 through 1966, the last complete year before the NHL expanded from six to twelve teams. Naturally the last category, Contemporary Greats, includes those who have played from 1967–68 through the present season.

Obviously I was unable to see any of the players in the eras of The Originals and The Prewar Aces. These picks were based on the opinions, research, and interviews of my co-editor, who has polled dozens of newspapermen, former players, coaches, managers, and other hockey people.

THE ORIGINALS

Goal: Lorne Chabot. In the mid-twenties it was fashionable to sign goaltenders who were small in stature on the theory that a half-pint goalie had more agility than a taller man. Montreal-born Chabot was the exception. He stood 6-1, weighed 185 pounds, and joined the original Rangers after playing for the Port Arthur (Ontario) Allan Cup champions. His averages in two seasons with New York were 1.56 and 1.79. In his second year Chabot was on the Stanley Cup-winners, although he suffered a serious eye injury and was replaced by Lester Patrick halfway through the series.

Defense: Ivan, "Ching," Johnson. It was Conn Smythe who wisely signed Johnson when assembling the Rangers in 1926. At 5-11, 210 pounds, the balding defenseman helped make the Rangers the hit of Broadway with his rugged, swashbuckling—at times crude—style of play. His nickname was a result of his inevitable grin following a successful bodycheck and his slitted eyes, which gave him the look of a Chinaman. Hence "Ching-a-ling," and finally Ching Johnson. A member of Hockey's Hall of Fame, Ching played for the Rangers for a decade, finishing his career after one season with the New York Americans.

Defense: Clarence, "Taffy," Abel. Like Johnson, Abel was imported from Minneapolis and teamed on the backline with Johnson to give the Rangers a defense that averaged 225 pounds and menaced enemy forwards at every turn. Taffy played three full seasons with New York, including the Cup-winning year 1928, before being traded to Chicago. While not quite as proficient as his buddy Ching, Taffy was an accomplished defenseman who meshed neatly with Johnson to give the Rangers an awesome pair of defenders.

Center: Frank Boucher. A big-league star before he came to the Rangers in their first season, Boucher played through the 1937–38 campaign and then made a brief comeback in 1943–44. His peerless playmaking gave the impression that Boucher had invented the art of passing and stickhandling. His all-round effectiveness was further enhanced by his obsessively clean play, which won him the Lady Byng Trophy seven times.

Left Wing: Fred, "Bun," Cook. The rugged member of the famed Cook–Boucher Line, Bun was frequently overshadowed by his more spectacular older brother, Bill, and the smoothy, Boucher. But Bun himself was a deft passer who could muck his way in the corners with the best of them. He was an original Ranger, playing on two Cup-winning teams. He was forced out of the lineup during the 1935–36 season by a recurring throat problem.

Right Wing: Bill Cook. Eddie Shore and Bill Cook were the two best players to move from the old Western League to the NHL. Shore went to Boston and Cook to the Rangers, where his stunning shots mummified goalies for a decade. When the Cook–Boucher line was broken up following Bun's departure, Bill was moved back to defense. He retired after the 1936–37 season, and eventually was voted into the Hall of Fame.

THE PREWAR ACES

Goal: Davie Kerr. Although he is associated with the Rangers, Kerr was actually signed by the Montreal Maroons in 1930 while playing on Montreal's Allan Cup champions. After several up and down seasons, Davie found his way in 1934 to New York, where he played splendidly for Lester Patrick. His peak came in the 1939–40 campaign, when he led the league in shutouts (eight), with a 1.60 goals-against average, and helped the Blueshirts to their last Stanley Cup victory. He played one more full season before retiring.

Defense: Walter, "Babe," Pratt, the ideal successor to Ching Johnson when the original defense work-horse had reached the end of his career. Pratt had a lovable disposition when he wasn't flattening the foe. He replaced Ching during the 1937 playoffs against Toronto and made headlines by scoring the winning goal in the deciding game. Babe remained a Ranger for seven years, starring on the 1940 Cup-winners and for the 1942 winners of the Prince of Wales Trophy. The next year he was dealt to Toronto, where he continued to excel and, as a result, was elected to the Hall of Fame.

Defense: Art Coulter. For reasons best known to the media, Art Coulter never achieved the acclaim that was bestowed upon more colorful types. But he was a winner to the core and proved it over a lengthy NHL career that started with the Chicago Black Hawks and ended with the Rangers. He came to New York in the middle of the 1935–36 season in a trade for Earl Siebert and made the second All-Star Team for three successive years. He was captain of the 1940 Stanley Cup champions and remained a Ranger until the conclusion of the 1941–42 season, when he enlisted in the U.S. Coast Guard and starred for the colorful Curtis Bay (Maryland) Cutters.

Center: Phil Watson. One of the most colorful Rangers, Watson was part of Lester Patrick's mid-thirties youth movement that rejuvenated the Blue-shirts. A fiery pivot, Watson first centered for Lynn Patrick and Cecil Dillon. Later Dillon was replaced by Bryan Hextall, and that unit terrorized the opposition for many years. Phil played for the 1940 Cup-winners and the 1942 first-place club. In 1943–44 he played for the Montreal Canadiens, returning to the Rangers the following year. He retired after the 1947–48 season.

Left Wing: Lynn Patrick. In order to convince his father, Lester, that he was qualified to play for the Rangers, Lynn had to be extra special. The figures prove that he was. He played regularly from the 1934–35 season through 1942–43 and returned after World War II for a last stint in 1945–46. Lynn reached his peak in 1940, when the Rangers won the Stanley Cup. He was named to the first All-Star Team in 1942 and to the second team in 1943.

Right Wing: Bryan Hextall. A hard-nosed native of Saskatchewan, Bryan twice led the NHL in goal-scoring and once in total points. He had a terrific burst of speed, was appropriately tough, and could stickhandle with the best of them. Like the Cook–Boucher line, the Hextall–Watson–Patrick unit dazzled the enemy with their stickwork until the outbreak of World War II depleted their ranks.

THE POSTWAR ERA

Goal: Chuck Rayner. Although he got his start with the New York Americans, Chuck Rayner achieved stardom with the Rangers, long after the Amerks had folded. He donned the blue shirt in 1945 and remained an honored member of the club until 1953. The spectacular and efficient nature of "Bonnie Prince Charley's" goaltending was matched only by his courage. Rayner's acclaimed split-saves enabled New York to reach the Stanley Cup finals in 1950, the year he won the Hart Trophy as the NHL's most valuable player. He never did win the Vezina Trophy, but that was no reflection on his ability, as attested to by players, coaches, and his election to the Hall of Fame.

Defense: Neil Colville. When he broke into the NHL with the prewar Rangers, Neil was a crack center on a line with his brother, Mac, and Alex Shibicky. Like so many aces, Neil had his career interrupted at its apex by wartime service. When he returned he realized he had slowed down (Mac and Alex were even slower), so he asked coach Frank Boucher if he could try playing defense. Boucher agreed and Neil emerged as one of the NHL's finest backliners. In the 1947–48 season the prematurely gray Colville led the Rangers back to the playoffs and made the second All-Star Team. He remained a valuable member of the squad until his retirement following the 1948–49 season.

Defense: Hy Buller. During the six-team era of the NHL, several outstanding skaters remained buried in the minors. When Boucher finally acquired Hy—one of the few Jewish skaters in the NHL—in 1951 from the Cleveland Barons' farm club, he was a seasoned pro who could play a solid defense yet bolster the attack with his hard shots from the blue line. His value was proven in his rookie season with election to the second All-Star Team. He retired prematurely after the 1953–54 campaign.

Center: Edgar Laprade. If ever there was a player who could emulate Frank Boucher's slick center-ice style it was Laprade, a sensational senior player in Port Arthur, Ontario, who had resisted Boucher's pleas to join his NHL club for several seasons. When the clean-playing Laprade finally did come to New York, he vindicated Boucher's judgment and bestowed a very special brand of class to the Blueshirts. He was a Ranger from his rookie year, 1945–46, through 1954–55.

Left Wing: Tony Leswick. The toy bulldog of the Blueshirts, Leswick made up in mustard what he lacked in polish and never failed to rebound from a boxing defeat to battle as hard as ever. He was also a very good scorer and was voted to the NHL's second All-Star Team in 1949–50. His best days were spent distracting the enemy from linemate Edgar Laprade so that Edgar could dipsy-doodle through their defenses. Leswick came to the Blueshirts in 1945–46 and remained a Ranger until he was traded to Detroit in 1951–52.

Right Wing: Andy Bathgate. The most popular Ranger in the late fifties and early sixties, Andy was the prize product of Boucher's Guelph (Ontario) junior team, which also spawned Dean Prentice, Lou

Fontinato, Aldo Guidolin, and Ron Murphy. After a bumpy start—he had been elevated to the NHL too quickly—Andy became a master stickhandler and one of the first successful proponents of the slapshot. It was one of Andy's shots that hit goalie Jacques Plante in the face, compelling Plante to don the first regularly worn face mask. Andy became a Ranger in 1952 and was traded to Toronto in February 1964 with Don McKenney in a highly controversial deal for Bob Nevin, Dick Duff, Arnie Brown, Rod Seiling, and Bill Collins.

CONTEMPORARY GREATS

Goal: Ed Giacomin. Like Bathgate, Giacomin suffered mightily in his early years as a Ranger. But he toughed it out under manager–coach Emile Francis' guidance and developed into one of the finest of the modern goaltenders. He is without peer as a stickhandling goalie.

Defense: Bill Gadsby. I am making a special exception here, listing Gadsby among the contemporaries although he left the Rangers in 1961. However, a place had to be found for this splendid performer who joined the Rangers from Chicago in 1954. He was a three-time member (1956, 1958 and 1959) of the NHL first All-Star Team. Like Buller, Gadsby took an efficient role on the offense but basically excelled in his own zone, especially when it came to blocking shots. He was the kingpin during the era of Phil Watson's coaching and is in the Hall of Fame.

Defense: Brad Park. I know it's a cliché, but Park

has been to the Rangers what Bobby Orr has been to the Bruins—a dynamo who can put the Blueshirts in the win column when he's operating at peak performance. His rapid development into a star—he made the first All-Star Team in his second season—has paralleled the Rangers' success.

Center: Jean Ratelle. A Ranger farmhand in the late fifties, when he skated for Guelph in the Ontario Hockey Association, Ratelle made it up from the minors in a slow but persistent climb. He reached his peak in the 1971–72 season, scoring 109 points, the most ever totaled by a Ranger. A season later he led the club in scoring again. He is a master craftsman from the cool, clean Boucher–Laprade school of hockey.

Left Wing: Vic Hadfield. In the 1971–72 season he scored fifty goals, removing any doubt that he had successfully made the transition from "policeman" to pointgetter. His 106 points that year were only three off the all-time club record, and his 142 penalty minutes attest to his competitive spirit. Vic was drafted from the Chicago Black Hawks in 1961 by Muzz Patrick, but didn't really develop into a productive scorer until the 1968–69 season.

Right Wing: Rod Gilbert. To many rooters he has been Mister Ranger because of his ability, glamor, and longevity. He played his first game in the blue shirt way back in the 1960–61 season and was the surprise star of the 1962 New York–Toronto playoff series. When Bathgate was dealt to Toronto, Gilbert was asked to fill his shoes at right wing. His ninety-seven and eighty-four points, respectively, in the past two seasons, suggest his value to the Ranger machine.

HONORABLE MENTION

I personally would not feel right if I failed to mention several other Rangers who brought us thrills down through the years but, for one reason or another, were omitted from my Great All-Time Team. So let's give due credit to the following:

Earl Seibert was a splendid defenseman in the early thirties and was a first team All-Star in 1935. From the same era, *Cecil Dillon* was a prolific right wing and an All-Star in 1937–38 after making the second team in 1935–36 and 1936–37. *Ott Heller,* an iron man if ever there was one, gained a second team berth on defense in 1940–41 and played energetically for New York many seasons after that.

Although he played most of his career with the Montreal Canadiens, center *Buddy O'Connor* never played better than in 1947–48, when he spurred the Rangers into the playoffs and was picked to the second All-Star Team. Another player who did most of his work in Montreal was defenseman *Doug Harvey.* Doug came to New York late in his playing life and left an indelible impression. As player–coach, he delivered a playoff berth for the Rangers and was also picked to the first All-Star Team.

When Harvey left New York, the top backliner on the squad was *Harry Howell*, a sturdy, cautious type who had been groomed on the same junior team as Andy Bathgate. Not surprisingly, Howell's closest friend was an extraordinary young man in his own right, *Camille Henry*. Skinny, fragile-looking, Henry was considered unfit to stand the rigors of NHL play. Yet he starred for several seasons as a power play specialist and general scoring threat and was named to the second All-Star Team in 1957–58.

Another left wing long admired by Ranger fans was *Dean Prentice,* a crony of Bathgate and Howell, who came to New York in the early fifties and stayed around until 1963. Few worked harder than "Deano," a forward who helped Bathgate accumulate his high point totals.

Last, but certainly not least, are three personal favorites of mine—*Don Raleigh, Wally Hergesheimer,* and *Andy Hebenton.*

Raleigh, a center, was called "Bones" because, like Henry, he was as thin as a rail. However, that had no effect on his stickhandling ability, which was enormous. He read and wrote poetry, lived alone out on Staten Island, and, of course, was the hero of the 1950 Stanley Cup final, even though the Rangers didn't win.

Hergesheimer, affectionately known as "Hergy," was a compact right wing who came to the Rangers by way of the Cleveland Barons. The bigger men—most players were bigger than Hergy—tirelessly tried to push him around, but the little guy kept coming back for more and was one of the best Ranger scorers in the early fifties.

One of the quietest men in sports, Hebenton was a right wing who worked up and down his wing almost always unnoticed until he would pop the puck in the net, which was often. He was a Ranger from 1955 through 1963 and is best remembered for scoring a sudden-death goal against Jacques Plante and the Canadiens on Garden ice.

Try as I might, I cannot guarantee my objectivity in making these selections. In some cases I must admit that I was inspired more by a gut reaction than cold statistics and I'll be the first to admit that there are three sides to every All-Star selection—your picks, my picks, and the deserving stars.

In any event this is the Albert's eye view of the best of the Blueshirts. I hope you liked them.

15. HOW TO WATCH AND ENJOY HOCKEY

Hockey is a very simple game to understand, as the late Dick Irvin, an eminently successful NHL coach, proved better than anyone. He called his players together one afternoon following a workout which was held because the team was in a severe scoring slump. Then he whispered something into the ears of his trainer and assistant trainer.

While the players wondered just what Irvin had in mind, the trainers removed one of the goal nets from the ice and paraded it into the dressing room. "Gentlemen," said Irvin, holding a puck in his hand, "this is the idea of the game." He took the puck, hurled it into the net, and walked out of the room. End of lesson about the simplicity of hockey.

The moral of this anecdote is simple enough: if you want to enjoy the game, always keep your eyes on the puck! That's as basic to the spectator as skating is to the player. Later on, when you've become a seasoned observer, you can train your eyes on other aspects of the game, but until then eyes-on-the-puck is the essential first step.

As any goaltender can tell you, following the

puck just isn't that easy anymore, although it used to be quite simple. Until Boom Boom Geoffrion introduced the slapshot to the NHL in the mid-fifties, the puck was nearly always visible to the fans' eyes.

But once Bobby Hull and Geoffrion popularized the slapshot, nearly every other big-leaguer got into the act, and that little black disc became increasingly difficult to follow. Almost overnight the hockey rink was changed from a fairly well-disciplined shooting gallery to one where the missiles gained more speed (from ninety to 120 m.p.h.) and less accuracy. Goalies, the most courageous of professional athletes, found their already difficult job virtually unbearable.

By the turn of the decade a style that could easily be called "contemporary hockey" had evolved. Nearly every player slapped the puck. Nearly every goalie had counterattacked by wearing the protective face mask. To contend with these "modern" developments, new offensive, defensive, and goaltending strategies had to be invented. To enjoy hockey, a fan should be reasonably familiar with these strategies.

The classiest to the eye and the one used by the Rangers accented passing and puck control. Whenever possible the club with the puck passes to a free teammate rather than simply shooting it into the enemy's corner of the rink and skating helter-skelter in an attempt to retrieve it. Never was the strategy of passing and puck control more emphasized than during the 1972 Team Canada-Russia series, where the Russians surprised and impressed everyone with their pass patterns.

There are, of course, several familiar variations on

the passing game. The Montreal Canadiens, traditionally a fleet group of skaters, are known for their "fire-wagon" brand of play. The imperative with the Canadiens is to "head-man" the puck, that is to continually pass it ahead to a man in motion so that he eventually will be able to outspeed or outmaneuver the defense.

Yvan Cournoyer of Montreal, one of the fastest skaters in the NHL, can be exploited in an assortment of ways by his center. Cournoyer will wait for the enemy defense to rush at his center, at which point he will be free to accept a pass.

Walt Tkaczuk of the Rangers has been learning the same tactic. A muscular center, Tkaczuk will often lure two players to him—he is so powerful it often requires two men to handle him—at which point he will shovel the puck to left wing Steve Vickers or right wing Bill Fairbairn. Occasionally Tkaczuk will use his wingmen as decoys. He did just that in the 1972 Cup semifinals against Chicago. The Black Hawks defenders, expecting Walter to pass either to his right or left, were caught napping as Tkaczuk cleverly bisected the backline and went in to score on goalie Tony Esposito.

And speaking of goalies, it would be wise to zero in on their styles for an intelligent approach to hockey watching. Like everything else about the game, goalie's styles have changed appreciably over the last three decades.

Prior to World War II, goaltending was basically a cut-and-dried art. "A goalie off his feet is helpless," said Lester Patrick, and thus a rule was established for decades. Only if a goaltender had to would he fall to the ice. If on his feet, he'd stop the puck with his glove hand or attempt the "splits," a spreadeagle kicking maneuver, if the puck was heading for either corner out of reach of his glove or stick. Since the puck was almost always visible in the prewar game, there was little else for a goalie to do but consider cutting down the angle on a breakaway—that is, move farther out of the net than normal to make it more difficult for the shooter to find the net's corners. Another specialized play was "stacking" the pads. A goalie would slide on his side, stacking one goal pad on top of the other to cover a large section of the net.

At the end of World War II hockey became speedier and involved a lot more scrambling. Shots that were once easy to follow were now becoming invisible because of the maze of bodies in front of the net. That type of terrifying shot—the "screened" shot—demanded a new defense, and several techniques were born.

Defensemen such as Bill Barilko of the Toronto Maple Leafs and Bob Goldham of the Detroit Red Wings began dropping in front of long shots from the blue line and found that they were successful acting as a second goaltender. In the meantime goaltenders were also changing their mode of play. To cope with the screened shot, Terry Sawchuk of the Red Wings decided that it was futile to look over the shoulders of players. Instead he developed a crouching style— never before used on a regular basis—in which he peered through the legs of the skaters to find the puck. The success of Sawchuk's system was evidenced by his amazingly low average and the fact that other goalies soon copied his style.

Sawchuk was succeeded in Detroit by Glenn Hall, who brought in a whole new technique which actually is the basis for the modern style of goaltending. Rather than try to peer between the legs, Hall decided that it was best to anticipate shots that would go for either corner. He did this by fanning his legs out into inverted "V" and dropping to his knees. Although Hall seemed to be playing goal in the manner of a five-year-old child, he demonstrated that by planting the points of his skates into the ice he could leap out of his "V" and scramble back to his feet into a normal goal-stopping position.

Younger goalies began patterning their style after Hall, and today virtually every goalie, with the exception of a few traditionalists frequently drop to their knees to block shots.

Some goalies, such as Eddie Giacomin of the Rangers, have furthered the responsibilities of the goaltender by becoming quarterback types, yelling strategy to their defensemen and forwards. The innovator of the quarterback technique was the most inventive goalie of all, Jacques Plante. "I learned the habit from Doug Harvey back in the 1950s," said Plante. "When I had control of the puck at the side of the net, for instance, and Harvey was coming back to pick it up, he'd want me to warn him which way to turn after he took the puck. He couldn't see what the checkers were doing behind him, but I could, and I'd tell him whether to turn around the net and cut straight down the ice or take a wider detour into the corner."

Today most players have learned the value of communication on the ice. Team Canada's last-minute hero, Paul Henderson, is one of the best shouters in the NHL. What he'll do is "hang" around the enemy blue line and watch for an opening, then shout for a pass and try to burst through the defense.

As I have mentioned before, defense has also undergone quite an evolution during the last decade. Today you will find three basic styles of play in the NHL, each style depending on the amount of time the defenseman spends on the attack.

Bobby Orr of the Bruins is the classic example of the offensive defenseman. Take a good look at Orr's stickhandling style sometime. He's so offense-oriented he frequently doesn't even bother to stickhandle the puck on the blade of his stick but merely pushes the rubber in front of him. This gives Bobby quite an advantage in speed and, surprisingly, puck control. If a defenseman tries to hit his stick, he won't get the puck —because the puck isn't on his stick, it's in front of him. And since the puck isn't on his blade, it's hard for the enemy to figure out which way he's going to turn.

There are few offensive defensemen like Orr, in fact, none. Brad Park and Pat Stapleton of Chicago do plenty of rushing, but for the most part they fall into a second category—defensemen who spend an equal amount of time on either side of the blue line. Guy Lapointe of Montreal is another like Park and Stapleton, whereas someone like Jim McKenny will rush at every opportunity.

The accent on speed and goal-scoring has made the third category—the defensive defenseman—more and more of a rarity. They are the unsung heroes of hockey, appreciated most by their goalies. Ed Van Impe of the Philadelphia Flyers, Ted Harris of the Minnesota North Stars, and Bill White of Chicago's Black Hawks are a few of the better defensive defense types. Their prime concern is keeping the enemy away from their net and not getting caught out of position. Few are more respected for this than Rod Seiling, a very underrated player who rarely gets the headlines. Rod's classy defense is appreciated more by the NHL players, who have to contend with him, and by his teammates than by the fans.

Defensive play is also important—and respected—in forwards. A skater such as Billy Fairbairn who frequently backchecks (retrieves the puck when the opposition is skating toward the Ranger net) is an invaluable asset to a team. A hockey skill that many offensemen have yet to learn is unselfishness. In his early NHL years Yvan Cournoyer had trouble becoming a regular because Montreal coach Toe Blake disapproved of his offense-only philosophy. "Yvan scored twenty goals one season," said Jacques Plante, "but it was mostly on the power play. He didn't work a regular shift because nobody had taught him how to switch to defensive play when his team lost the puck."

It was defense-oriented forwards such as Fairbairn, Tkaczuk, and Vickers who helped bottle up Bobby Orr in the 1973 New York–Boston playoff. The Rangers first studied films of Orr in action and then had Park imitate Orr's style in workouts before the Cup round began.

"The movies taught us that it would be best to

flood his side of the rink," Giacomin told me. "With that in mind we kept shooting the puck into Orr's corner so that he had to go back and retrieve it. Eventually even Orr got tired and his game slowed down. It was just what we had hoped would happen."

Needless to say, you can't win hockey games without scoring goals, so it's worthwhile to learn the little nuances that make a great scorer great. Take Jean Ratelle of New York. He has mastered the wrist shot, which is more accurate than the wild slapshot and quicker to release. But he also has learned how to shoot the puck off his "wrong" leg. To understand this you must remember that a shooter usually fires the puck off his opposite leg—thus a right-handed player will shoot off his left leg. Ratelle, however, has enhanced his scoring ability by being able to pull the trigger with either foot forward.

No discussion of scorers would be complete without mentioning Phil Esposito of the Bruins. Some critics have accused him of scoring "garbage" goals because he stations himself in the "keyhole" about twenty feet in front of the net and waits for his linemates to feed him a pass. But Esposito does much more than that. He's a superb stickhandler and uses his bulk to his best advantage while circling a defenseman.

Esposito's teammate Derek Sanderson is a master of another important art—winning face-offs. It requires terrific reflexes and a bit of psychology, not to mention lots of practice. Derek has said that he spent years perfecting his face-off technique, and his results prove it has been time well spent.

While on the subject of strategy, psychological and

otherwise, it is important to consider the question of how much science is involved in a hockey game. Certainly not as much as in football, where game plans and individual plays have become increasingly complicated. But hockey is not a simple-minded game either. The Rangers power play—when they have a man advantage—is as scientific an effort as anything devised by George Allen, the great football coach. Likewise, the Rangers penalty-killing team, led by Fairbairn and Tkaczuk, has also worked out a few clever plays to keep the puck away from the enemy until the Rangers regain full strength.

One way to watch a hockey game—a method my broadcasting chores seldom permit me to use—is to concentrate on one specific aspect of the game. When I am on my own time I always enjoy concentrating on the goaltender. Try fastening your gaze on Ed Giacomin next time you're at a Ranger game, especially when the other team has a power play going and he is facing the most difficult shots. Eddie once helped me better understand the art of goaltending by telling me about the strong and weak sides of a goalie.

"The side where the goalie holds his stick," said Giacomin, "is his weak side. It automatically becomes his weak side because he can't catch the puck with that hand, since he's holding the stick in it. So he's limited to the back of his glove for deflecting the puck and his skate. On the strong side he has his skate for the low shots and his trapper's glove for the high ones."

Eddie explained that every goalie tries to capitalize on his strong side by enticing the shooter. "We give the shooter more room on the strong side," Eddie explained. "We hope that he'll go for the bait and then, at the last second, we'll try to cover up."

Like most of the older pros, Giacomin plays his "angles" as much as possible. If, for example, Yvan Cournoyer skates in alone on Eddie, the goalie will try to cut down the angle. "The more I move out," Giacomin told me, "the bigger I become in the shooter's eyes and the smaller the net looks to him."

Of course there's always the danger that a wily skater like Cournoyer will fake a shot and try to circle around Giacomin and put the puck in the vacant net. "When that happens," said Eddie, "I try to use my stick to jab the puck away from him, or use my leg to block the shot."

Enjoying a hockey game also requires a certain amount of "work" on the part of the fan. Good spectating, like good playing, doesn't come easy. By good spectating I mean rooting for your favorite team, but also being fair to the opposition—and the officials.

Hockey is a game of mistakes; it has to be because it is so fast. The athletes are playing with artificial feet (skates), and artificial arms (sticks) on an artificial surface (ice). Since mistakes are inevitable, I believe the fans should try to be as understanding as possible. Everyone goofs at one time or another, so let's not be too brutal with the offender. And let's remember that the referee is one of the very, very few impartial people in the arena.

Criticism is fine as long as it does not become too negative, too abusive, and as long as it doesn't ruin the enjoyment of the event for you, the fan.

So the next time you're out at the Garden, take a few minutes to watch Giacomin's goaltending; notice how much time the defensemen spend on the attack; watch for moves of unselfishness on the part of the players; and see if your overall enjoyment of the game doesn't improve.

16. PROFESSIONAL HOCKEY BROADCASTING

I wasn't even born when the first hockey game went over the airways, and the chances are neither were you—unless you're over fifty years old.

The dean and originator of hockey play-by-play is Foster Hewitt of Toronto who, at this writing, is still handling the Toronto Maple Leafs' games just as efficiently as he was back in the Roarin' Twenties, when this business began.

From time to time we "moderns" tend to gripe about the condition of our play-by-play facilities. But whenever I feel like griping I simply recall stories that Hewitt has told me about the way it was when he began.

The year was 1923. Radio was in its infancy, television was still a dream, and those few lucky people who could listen to the game did so on crude crystal sets. Hewitt was only eighteen years old at the time, a young reporter at the *Toronto Daily Star*. But the *Star*'s radio editor, Basil Lake, realized the potential of the medium and suggested that young Foster take a crack at reporting a hockey game over the air.

The first hockey game ever broadcast was an amateur match between Toronto's Parkdale club and a team from Kitchener, Ontario. Conditions at the Mutual Street Arena in Toronto were horrible, to say the least. Hewitt was stationed in a glass-enclosed booth that was continually fogged-up. The players looked like a collection of skating phantoms.

Despite the problems, Hewitt *did* manage to report the complete game, and more important, the public was enthusiastic about the job he did—so much so that radio station CFCA made hockey broadcasts a part of its regular programming and Hewitt moved on to handling the NHL games.

Because he was the first and because he was good, Hewitt became the model for most hockey broadcasters who followed. His high-pitched voice would reach a unique crescendo as a player released his shot, and Foster would shout, "HE SHOOTS!" followed by the inevitable climax when the red light went on—"HE SCORES!!" There has never been anything quite like Hewitt's delivery and, I daresay, there never will be.

He was—and is—the Babe Ruth of hockey broadcasting. But the passing of Ruth did not mean that nobody else hit home runs and, likewise, Hewitt has not remained the only outstanding hockey play-by-play broadcaster. Doug Smith of Montreal became the first outstanding broadcaster of Canadiens' games, followed by Danny Gallivan, who still airs the Montreal matches.

Foster's son, Billy Hewitt, has been doing games out of Toronto for several years and, not surprisingly, projects a style very much like his father's.

In New York old-time Rangers' fans will recall Bert

Lee and Ward Wilson who handled the games and color on WHN (later WMGM)'. To give them full credit, they did not ape Hewitt in any way and introduced several nuances that made Rangers' games unusually interesting.

Wilson, who was an accomplished raconteur, would visit the Rangers' dressing room after each game, win-or-lose, and interview the players either before or after they had showered. The Blueshirts were considerably less than the best in those days, but Wilson never failed to come up with a lively interview. By far his most difficult night was on January 23, 1944, when the Rangers played the Red Wings at Olympia Stadium in Detroit. The home team scored fifteen goals in that game and the Rangers none! Can you imagine what a time Wilson must have had in the dressing room that night?

Lee and Wilson were the first hockey broadcasters I ever heard. I was ten years old at the time and became so enthralled with the play-by-play that I went to the sporting goods store in the Manhattan Beach section of Brooklyn, where I lived, and bought a hockey scoresheet. The broadcasts really stimulated my interest in the game, and soon I was playing hockey on roller skates right in the middle of Kensington Street —a routine that didn't quite please my mother.

We placed the nets—made out of screens—in the middle of the gutter and kept them there until a car came along. Then we'd move them to the sidewalk, putting them back in place after the car went by. Needless to say, that wasn't enough for me, or my younger brothers, Al and Steve. We also set up a goal cage in the basement of our house. That's when I got my first lesson in just how rough hockey can be.

My brother Al took a slapshot with the makeshift wooden puck we had been using, and I made the save. The only trouble was that the puck hit me right where it hurts most. I wasn't wearing a protective cup! That was my first realization that hockey might be more enjoyable, not to mention safer, from a broadcasting booth.

I decided that I would try an interview with a real, live big-league hockey player and have it printed in my school paper. My father told me that this would be a long-shot, but I got in touch with Herb Goren, who was then the Rangers publicity man and who had grown up in Brooklyn like myself. To my amazement, Goren agreed to arrange for me to meet two Rangers—Don Raleigh and Andy Bathgate. Even more thrilling was the fact that Goren's friend Howard Cosell happened to be there at the time and overheard my interview. It was one of those cases of being in the right place at the right time.

Cosell had just launched a program called "All-League Clubhouse"—a kids sports show—and needed one more panelist. I was elected and became a regular on the show for two years. I learned an awful lot about broadcasting, although it wasn't the precise kind of broadcasting that interested me.

Play-by-play was my interest, and the only way to get exposure in this area was to get close to a play-by-play broadcaster. In those days the Rangers had a farm team in the Eastern League called the Rovers who played at Madison Square Garden on Sunday afternoons. Whenever possible I would climb up to the radio press box at the Rover games and stand as close to the broadcasters as possible. Knowing the broadcasters and reporters was as vital to me at the time as knowing the players.

At each game I'd follow the action and, *sotto voce,* would do a "simulcast" of my own. That was fun for a while, but I wanted to do more; and my father realized this. When I was thirteen years old he presented me with a tape recorder, which really turned things around for me. I started practicing my hockey play-by-play right from my own room. My window fronted our roller hockey court, so I'd prop myself up and do play-by-play of the games down on the street below.

My father helped me in other ways, mostly because he loved hockey as much as I did. Eventually I graduated from the Sunday afternoon Rovers games to the Sunday night Rangers games at the Garden, but not without a little pain.

One night my father decided to take me to see the Rangers play the Canadiens, which, to my mind, was as good as going to the World Series. When we got out of the subway at Eighth Avenue and 50th Street, there was a terrific crowd, and that worried me. We finally pushed our way to the box office, where all I could hear was this voice coming over the loudspeaker, "All tickets for tonight's game are sold out. There are no more tickets available."

I felt like crying right on the spot, and I suspect my father realized this. He took me by the hand and said we'd see something just as good—and he was right. We walked over to Broadway and went to the movies at the Astor Theater. The film was *The Jackie Robinson Story*.

By age fourteen I knew in my heart that there was only one career in store for me and that was radio and television broadcasting, and I made up my mind that I had to gear my life to reach that goal. Saying this now sounds a little preposterous, since the odds were pretty heavy against it. But the breaks started falling my way.

First I got a job with the old Brooklyn Dodgers as an office boy. Part of the payment was a pair of tickets to the games at Ebbets Field. I would bring along my tape recorder and practice the play-by-play. To complement my broadcasting, I worked hard on my writing. I learned early in life that the best way to learn something is to *do* it. So I wrote for the newspaper at Abraham Lincoln High School and got more experience.

In the winter months hockey and basketball were my favorite sports, but basketball presented more opportunities at the time. My friends and I organized a Jim Baechtold Fan Club in honor of one of the New York Knickerbockers, and soon we helped organize a New York Knicks Fan Club, of which I became president and editor of its official paper.

That was a key break for me because it enabled me to meet some people around the Garden. Knicks players got to know me, and soon members of the Knicks front office began to recognize the skinny kid from Brooklyn. One of those officials was John Goldner, who got me a job as ball boy for the Knicks. For the first time I really got inside the dressing rooms and next to the big-leaguers. It was a revelation because I got to see the human side of the athletes and learned that some of them were first-rate grouches and others were as wonderful as I had hoped they would be. But working for the Knicks actually helped me improve my hockey broadcasting.

Goldner gave me permission to sit in the press box during Rangers games and also said it was okay for me to take my tape recorder along. Today, with press box space at a premium, I would have had a hard time even getting close to rink side. But in those years the Rangers weren't selling out every game and there was room in the press box for amateurs like myself.

After each Rangers game I'd return home and compare my play-by-play with the job I had done during the previous game. After that I would compare my style with those of the great Canadian broadcasters Foster Hewitt and Danny Gallivan, whose voices I had preserved on tape.

By the time I reached my senior year in high school I actually felt I was a professional announcer, although I had not yet received a penny for broadcasting and wouldn't for several years to come. In the interim I would go on to college, where I could perfect my writing and broadcasting technique and perhaps even get a job doing some radio work. I decided to seek out a smaller city where opportunities would be better than in New York. So in 1959 I headed for Syracuse University and hoped for the best. Once again I got all the required breaks and my career was really and truly in orbit.

Syracuse was the perfect place for me. It had a

minor-league baseball club in the International League and a basketball team in the NBA and a fine university with just enough journalism courses to suit me. I managed to get a job as a disk jockey on one of the local radio stations and became an announcer for the baseball team. My hockey broadcasting experience suffered somewhat because Syracuse didn't have a professional team at the time. That may account for my early dissatisfaction with my hockey play-by-play technique. I talked too much on my early hockey games because I was having difficulty finding my rhythm. I was giving hockey more of a basketball call.

It was then that I discovered the major difference between handling hockey and basketball on the radio. Basketball is much easier to broadcast. The pace of a basketball game is fast, but the action is steady, allowing the announcer to anticipate the play-by-play. By contrast, hockey has too many "bang-bang" situations to lend itself to an easy broadcasting pattern.

In Syracuse one opportunity after another presented itself. I handled classical music for one FM station and rock 'n roll for another, in addition to the baseball. But my eyes and heart were on New York, and in 1963 the call that I had been hoping and waiting for finally came through. It was sportscaster, Marty Glickman, offering me a spot as his back-up man and writer. I had met Marty during my days as Knick ball boy and he had taken interest in my broadcasting hopes. I accepted, took the first train to New York, and finished my last year of college at New York University.

Once again basketball proved to be my *entrée* into

hockey. As Glickman's sidekick I merely had to bide my time until he missed a game and I was called in to pinch-hit on WCBS Radio. The break came when Marty was off on a trip to Europe and was scheduled to return in time to handle a Knicks-Celtics game in Boston Garden. Glickman's Paris–New York flight was delayed by poor weather conditions and I was called in to handle the broadcast. I did a good enough job to win Marty's trust. Not long after that I worked a Knicks–Pistons game in Detroit which was followed by a Rangers–Red Wings game. Since the games were back to back, the station manager suggested that I remain in Detroit and take a crack at the NHL game. It was a dream come true. But looking back on my first hockey broadcast, it would be more accurate to describe it as a nightmare.

It was a frightening experience. My fear was rooted in the simple fact of inexperience. I knew basketball but I was a newcomer to the world of hockey. The rink seemed enormous compared to a basketball court. The climb to Olympia Stadium's broadcast booth for that Red Wings–Rangers game was no lark either. The booth itself was like a closet, and hid both the scoreboard and the clocks. In order to see them I had to look through a periscope. I felt as if I was broadcasting the game from the inside of a submarine!

The game was a disaster. Detroit completely dominated the Rangers, winning something like 9–4. To my surprise, I thought I did a pretty good job, but rehearing it ten years later was a frightful experience. My rhythm was good but I could tell that I didn't capture the flow of play the way I had hoped I would. In plain English, I was nervous.

When they asked me to do another Rangers game, I felt a lot better. Some of the first-game butterflies were gone and I thought I was rather cool, all things considered. I handled one more game that season and then went back to the drawing board, so to speak, to analyze my flaws. My play-by-play was fast-paced, but I was still looking for my rhythm. In addition, I felt I wasn't capturing the "intangibles," things like the intensity and the pace of the game, the philosophies of the respective teams, and the "angles" that make each game different from the rest.

But it was a start, and in the meantime I continued to look for openings. I moved from WCBS to WHN, where I became sports director, and it was there that I sold the idea of having Rangers home and away games broadcast all season. The station's directors liked the idea and managed to obtain both the Knicks and Rangers games, which I handled.

Now, after more than a decade of broadcasting hockey, I have hit on my own formula—if there is such a thing—for first-rate hockey broadcasting. Like anything else, it requires constant homework. A man just doesn't walk into the radio booth and, by osmosis, become a pro. Homework means reading all the newspapers, including the out-of-town papers, the weekly and monthly sporting publications, and the official NHL releases. This enables the broadcaster to follow the flow of players and to keep up with trends and other information that would be interesting to the listeners.

The most important technical matter to master is memorization of various team rosters. A broadcaster must be able to instantly recognize a player by the number on his back or by his appearance. Occasionally numbers are useless to the broadcaster. Up until 1972 I handled the Rangers games from a location near the Madison Square Garden roof, where it was nearly impossible to pick out the numbers. I had to be able to recognize the players by their hair styles, their hair color, or any other aspect of their physique that distinguished them from the next player.

Mastering the identification of players is basic, as skating is to playing hockey. The nuances are what make the difference between the average announcer and the very special ones. Repetition of phrases, overuse of words, exaggeration—these are all marks of the mediocre play-by-play man.

An announcer who uses the expression "great" too often diminishes the value of the adjective and clouds its meaning for the listener. The better broadcaster finds synonyms for "excellence" and sprinkles them throughout his description.

I used to get hung up on certain expressions, such as "flip" or "throw the puck," until I replayed the tapes of my broadcasts and detected the mistakes. Another mistake I made during the 1972–73 season was overusing the phrase "loose in the corner." Several fans told me they kept thinking I was talking about Don Luce, the former Ranger, now with the Buffalo Sabres, and they pictured Luce in the corner.

Which brings us to one of the most sensitive areas of

radio journalism, the problem of subjectivity, or rooting for the home team while handling the game.

It is a problem for the most expert announcer because hockey fans are the most passionate of rooters and interpret the slightest tremor in a broadcaster's voice as meaningful. If, for example, I described a player on the Boston Bruins as a "cheap-shot artist," chances are the Rangers fans will commend me, Bruins fans will call me a "homer," and heaven knows what a Pittsburgh fan might think. I try very, very hard to be impartial and to give credit where credit is due. But sometimes the inflections of my voice give away more about my personal feelings than I would like them to.

Take the Rangers–Bruins playoff series of April 1973. As the Rangers took the Bruins in five games, I found myself being swept up by the emotion of the series. When all is said and done, I am a fan, which isn't all that bad because being a fan injects enthusiasm into the broadcast. Just like the players, I was psyched-up for the games.

Yet, as enthusiastic as I was during the series, I made an effort when Boston scored to shout "HE SCORES!" just as loudly and as excitedly—I think—as I did for the Rangers. If a broadcaster loses sight of his objectivity, he may ruin the game for some of the fans.

I am not suggesting that I am perfect, but after more than ten years on the job I believe I am in a position to give advice to potential broadcasters. The following are answers to the questions most frequently asked of me:

Is it necessary to have played the game of hockey in order to become a hockey announcer?

I think it helps—but is not totally necessary. My active playing career was limited to four years of roller hockey—highlighted by two significant events. The high point of my career, scoring eight goals in one game to break a Kensington Street (Brooklyn, New York) record, was one of them. The other was the low point of my career. In the sudden-death overtime of a final playoff game, I found myself with the puck on my stick and one defenseman to beat. I faked the defenseman out of position, utilizing a very tricky hip shift and shoulder feint, while switching my stick from left to right. Now it was Marv Albert versus the goaltender.

I zoomed in . . . would I lift it over his shoulder or fake him out of position? The decision was made for me a split-second later as I lost my right roller skate.

What is the toughest facet of a hockey game to call?

I don't have anything against the Toronto Maple Leafs, but their style of play provides the most difficult times because they persist in holding the puck in their own zone—passing it back and forth—playing, for the most part, a defensive game. This *is* good hockey, but it's easier to call the play-by-play for an attacking-style club.

Where is the most difficult place to broadcast a hockey game?

Although the Rangers have had pretty good luck at Chicago Stadium, I've found Chicago's broadcast facilities a drawback. First of all, you must be in excellent physical shape to reach the booth, which is some

212 steps upward. Usually, in handling hockey play-by-play, I try to concern myself with the physical features of the individual players—you get to know them quite well during the season. But in Chicago, because you're so far from the ice, even numbers are difficult to see. In addition to this, the time clock is impossible to read at a quick glance on the broadcast level, the public-address system is muffled, and, at times, I have felt that the booth, suspended from the ceiling, is in danger of collapsing. It rumbles and sways as the game progresses.

How would you compare broadcasting hockey on radio to doing it on TV?

In most other sports the television play-by-play is easier to handle than radio because the picture tells the story. But in hockey, because of the nature of the game (the great speed and no clear possession of the puck), TV has more problems.

From the announcing viewpoint it is more a question of restraint, because the announcer can fall into two traps: talking too much or talking too little. On radio, with no picture to aid the viewer, the play-by-play man can find his own style and not be influenced by the camera pickup.

Since you have two brothers who are both big-league sports announcers, is there any rivalry or jealousy among the three of you?

Rivalry, yes. Jealousy, no. In fact I am enormously proud of them. I have listened to Steve's Cleveland Crusaders' broadcasts and Al's New York Nets' and New York Islanders' play-by-play, and I can honestly say they have made it, not because their name is Albert, but because they are good. Of course we have our friendly rivalries, and whenever the opportunity to needle one another presents itself, you can bet we jump at the chance. To give you an example, here is the transcript of a recent interview, with Pete Alfano of *Newsday*, in which both Al and I were asked to participate:

QUESTION: We're on the air. Are the Alberts from New York or did you migrate here from the Dutch West Indies?

MARV: Our family is from Manhattan Beach in Brooklyn and our parents still live there.

AL: Do you want the exact address?

MARV: Ignore him. Al has been an outpatient from a psychiatric ward for a number of years. I'm now living in Woodmere, Long Island.

AL: I live in Forest Hills, Queens.

QUESTION: At what age did you first become interested in becoming broadcasters?

MARV: As the most serious member of the family, I first became interested in the fifth grade, or ever since I first watched Ray Felix. I was given a tape recorder and took it to games, where I practiced play-by-play. Al and I even started a Knicks fan club. Al sealed the envelopes.

AL: We set up a press box in the den and we called our station WMPA. Those are Marv's initials. We had a crowd-reaction record and I handled that while Marv did the broadcasts.

MARV: It was Al's first breakthrough as an outpatient.

QUESTION: Were either of you athletes of any distinction while in school?

MARV: I was strictly schoolyard. I couldn't go to my left. I went to Syracuse University and worked for the station up there. I never fooled myself. There was no way I could play pro sports.

AL: I was a goalie at Ohio University, an excellent one by college standards. The Rangers invited me to summer camp in 1968 and I spent a week there.

MARV: Emile Francis has a good sense of humor.

QUESTION: How did you do?

AL: I was assigned to the farm team in Toledo of the International League. But I became overpsyched. Then I got tendonitis in my knee. In my first exhibition game I came out of the net to stop a two-on-nothing break and shot the puck off my own defenseman. It rolled into the net. I knew I was going into broadcasting eventually, so after two months I quit and announced their games.

QUESTION: Were you hesitant about coming to New York and being known only as Marv Albert's brother?

AL: Our backgrounds are the same, so the similarities are going to be there. But I don't imitate Marv. I knew what I could do. Being his brother didn't bother me.

QUESTION: What announcers did both of you try to emulate when you were growing up?

AL: As a kid I used to listen to Marv on the radio.

MARV: Graham McNamee was my favorite. Really, I guess I listened to Marty Glickman and Les Keiter. When I first went on the air I was a carbon copy of

Marty. I even did the commercials the same. I became my own man when I went to WHN.

QUESTION: Should an announcer be objective or is he allowed the liberty of rooting for the home team?

MARV: I have this thing about being objective. And the Knicks and Rangers let me say what I want. Of course they're winning clubs. I have gotten overemotional a few times, like when Willis Reed walked on the court for the seventh game of the championship. But I go wild when I hear announcers say "we" or "us."

AL: Some announcers go to extremes. I believe objectivity lends credibility to the broadcast.

QUESTION: What do your parents think of your choice of career?

AL: They really let us do what we wanted to. They have a radio in every room, and one night they had all three of us on the air at once. It makes my mother happy, because she always knows where we are.

QUESTION: Do both of you feel secure, or do you worry about your ratings?

MARV: I was a little awed when I first started. But now I feel very much secure, even though there's little security in this business. There are plenty of jobs open for young sportscasters, especially in hockey with all those expansion teams.

AL: I never worry about losing my job. I never give it much thought.

QUESTION: Since you're both secure, you probably won't mind telling us the biggest flub you made since entering broadcasting?

MARV: Arranging this interview. That, and in 1961 when I did a recreation of the Syracuse Chiefs baseball games, I left out three innings of a Chiefs–Buffalo game. What's worse, there wasn't one phone call.

AL: I really can't recall anything, not that you would be interested in.

QUESTION: What sport do you prefer, basketball or hockey?

MARV: It depends on how the team is going.

AL: It's difficult when a team loses so much as the Islanders. I miss not seeing the Knicks and Rangers.

QUESTION: Which of you is the better announcer?

MARV: Steve.

AL: Steve.

MARV: Actually, I get a kick listening to Steve do the Crusaders' games. He is poised and has been around the business. He has a good opportunity there.

What is your schedule on broadcast day?

MARV: Here's a typical Sunday for a home game:

Ironically, my eating habits are similar to those of a player. I will eat a substantial pre-game meal around 2 p.m. for a 7 p.m. contest. I'm always wound up on the day of a game, and when I feel the butterflies I know all is right. Former Oakland goaltender Charley Hodge once told me: "If I didn't feel the butterflies I'd begin to worry. When you're nervous, you care."

However, unlike the players, about an hour before game time, I usually sneak in a malted. This has become a weekly ritual; without that malted my stomach usually talks to me during the second period.

At 6 p.m. I drop by the Ranger Executive Office to chat with manager Emile Francis and publicist John Halligan. They bring me up to date on late developments. Then, armed with two cups of water, I proceed to the radio booth.

As I enter the booth, all is still dark. The early arrivals are filtering in and the organist has just begun to hit the keyboard. An extra-early arrival is the engineer, Harry, "Homerun," Baker, who has already spent some two hours setting up equipment.

At 6:15 the statistician arrives. He and I pore over the statistical sheets and check the commercial lineup.

At 6:30 both clubs make their warmup appearances, and I identify each opposing player aloud to refamiliarize myself. Some players will cause more trouble than others during the course of play-by-play for no particular reason; these troublesome names are repeated over and over.

At 6:45 the names of the referee and linesmen are announced. Back at the studios a newscast is being completed.

At 6:59:45 an announcer says: "Now to Madison Square Garden for Ranger Hockey with Marv Albert . . ."

Then, at 7 p.m., the engineer gives the signal, the mike is open . . . "Good evening everyone. From Madison Square Garden . . ."

17. THE LISTENERS WRITE

One of the most difficult aspects of being behind a microphone, either doing play-by-play or handling a radio show such as "Sportsline," is the fact that I never get an opportunity to actually *see* my listening audience.

This, of course, creates a certain block between announcer and audience, but it is one which frequently is overcome in the mails. I am fortunate in the sense that my listeners like to write. In fact they *love* to write. I wouldn't be surprised if the post office gave me my own zip code.

Often the fans make extremely insightful comments about my work and the performance of the Rangers or individual players.

These letters I enjoy very much.

But there is another group of letters which I enjoy even more. They are the funny ones; the mail that either deliberately or otherwise is downright amusing.

A letter I received a year ago started with the

writer saying that he was a big Ranger fan, and as a result he had named his two sons after Dave Balon and myself. Feeling quite flattered, I continued to read the letter, which said: "Little Dave is four years old and his brother, Mark, is two." Only then did I look at the salutation, which read, "Dear Mark Alpert."

This started me thinking about some of the humorous letters I have received from Ranger fans over the years. The humor is usually quite unintentional.

Many of the people are quite anxious to learn as much as they can about the personal lives of the players. Consider the lady who wrote me of her love for the team. She would drive up and down the streets of Long Beach, where most of the Rangers live, hoping to get a glimpse of a player.

One day she was stopped by a policeman who had noticed her previously driving around the neighborhood without any apparent destination. As a result of this encounter, she discontinued the practice. However, she wrote me to find out if I knew of any houses for sale in that area.

Other letters might be better appreciated preserved in their original form. Consider the following:

Dear Marv:

I wonder if you can give me some advice. I am a big Ranger fan and dream of playing for them some day. I am sixteen years old and I have one problem. I grew up in the south and I don't know how to ice skate yet. If I take lessons and learn a little, do you think that I could be a goalie? They don't do much skating.

Dear Marv:

I live in North Carolina and I have just started to pick up your broadcasts. Because of the static I can't really tell which sport you are broadcasting. It sounded like it might be hockey, and I am a big hockey fan, so please let me know if it is hockey so I can try to get a better radio.

Dear Marv:

I would like to buy my brother a real hockey uniform for Christmas. Can you let me know if any of the Rangers are getting new ones and might want to sell their old ones?

Dear Marv:

I am sixteen years old and my ambition is to be a sports announcer. Could you please give me some advice about colleges? I would like to do the Ranger games, so I hope you won't be mad when I take away your job.

Dear Marv:

Can you please send me an autographed picture? I saw you in person at Madison Square Garden. You look much better in pictures than you do in person.

Dear Marv:

I enjoy your Ranger broadcasts on WNBC, but being a very nervous person I find it difficult to listen to the final buzzer at the end of each period. It alarms me. Can you have your engineering staff bleep it out? Or perhaps you can cut away to the studio when the buzzer goes off.

Dear Marv:

I think you are a spectacular announcer. Please send me two tickets to next Sunday's Ranger–Boston game.

The humor in other letters often comes as a result of inadvertent grammatical errors. One fan asked a question concerning Emile Francis and Gilles Villemure. His next sentence was, "If you could send them to me in two months I would appreciate it very much." Somehow I don't think that Gilles and Emile would have been as appreciative. One inquisitive young lady wanted to know if "the players are allowed to bring parts of their families to games FREE?" I started to write her back and say "just the arms and the legs." A young man was interested in starting a fan club and asked me for information, because "I would like to know more about the club I would like to start."

It's always enjoyable to receive fan mail and, as one who used to write autograph request letters to athletes, I can appreciate how important it is to respond. Sometimes, as you can see, it is difficult to provide a feasible answer. However, I have yet to sink to the depths of a popular New York disc jockey, Don Imus, who closes his program each morning by imploring his listeners to "KEEP THOSE CARDS AND LETTERS!"

MIKE SHAYNE MYSTERIES
by Brett Halliday

*More than 30 million Mike Shayne
mysteries have been printed
in Dell Book editions alone!*

ARMED . . . DANGEROUS . . . 60c
THE CARELESS CORPSE 75c
CAUGHT DEAD 75c
FIT TO KILL 60c
GUILTY AS HELL 60c
THE HOMICIDAL VIRGIN 75c
I COME TO KILL YOU 60c
KILL ALL THE YOUNG GIRLS 75c
MERMAID ON THE ROCKS 60c
MURDER IN HASTE 60c
MURDER SPINS THE WHEEL 60c
NEVER KILL A CLIENT 75c
PAY OFF IN BLOOD 75c
A REDHEAD FOR MIKE SHAYNE 75c
SHOOT TO KILL 75c
SO LUSH, SO DEADLY 60c

If you cannot obtain copies of these titles from your local bookseller, just
send the price (plus 15c per copy for handling and postage) to Dell Books,
Post Office Box 1000, Pinebrook, N. J. 07058.

26 Weeks on *The New York Times* Bestseller List!
"Terrifying, suspenseful, mind shattering."
Washington Post

DELIVERANCE

by James Dickey

This novel, by one of America's finest poets, is a tale of violent adventure and inner discovery. Four men embark on a canoe trip down a wild section of a river in the heartland of today's South. When two of the group are attacked viciously and perversely by mountaineers, a mildly adventurous canoe trip explodes into a gruesome nightmare of horror and murder.

"The limit of dramatic tension . . . a novel that will curl your toes!" *The New York Times*

Now a major motion picture from
Warner Brothers starring Burt Reynolds and
Jon Voight

A DELL BOOK $1.25

HOW MANY OF THESE
DELL BESTSELLERS
HAVE YOU READ?

1. **THE MAN WHO LOVED CAT DANCING**
   by Marilyn Durham $1.75

2. **LAST TANGO IN PARIS** by Robert Alley $1.75

3. **THE BRAND-NAME CARBOHYDRATE GRAM
   COUNTER** by Corinne T. Netzer $1.50

4. **THE EROTIC LIFE OF THE AMERICAN WIFE**
   by Natalie Gittelson $1.75

5. **GEORGE S. KAUFMAN** by Howard Teichmann $1.95

6. **THE TRUTH ABOUT WEIGHT CONTROL**
   by Dr. Neil Solomon $1.50

7. **MEAT ON THE HOOF** by Gary Shaw $1.50

8. **MAFIA, USA** by Nicholas Gage $1.75

9. **THE HAPPY HOOKER** by Xaviera Hollander $1.50

10. **THE WATER IS WIDE** by Pat Conroy $1.50

11. **THE OSTERMAN WEEKEND** by Robert Ludlum $1.50

12. **11 HARROWHOUSE** by Gerald A. Browne $1.50

13. **DISRAELI IN LOVE** by Maurice Edelman $1.50

14. **WILL THERE REALLY BE A MORNING?**
    by Frances Farmer $1.50

15. **A PSYCHIATRIST'S HEAD**
    by Martin Shepard, M.D. $1.50

16. **DEEP THROAT** by D. M. Perkins $1.50

If you cannot obtain copies of these titles from your local bookseller, just send the price (plus 15c per copy for handling and postage) to Dell Books, Post Office Box 1000, Pinebrook, N. J. 07058.